HUNGARIAN DOG BREEDS

PÁL SÁRKÁNY
IMRE ÓCSAG
Hungarian Dog Breeds

CORVINA

Original Hungarian revised by **Csaba Anghi**
Translated by **Martha Egri Richardson** and **Yvonne Hajdú**
Translation revised by **Kay White** and **Christina Molinari**

Second, revised edition
First edition published in 1977 under the title
"Dogs of Hungary", Corvina Kiadó, Budapest
© Pál Sárkány and Imre Ócsag, 1986
ISBN 963 13 2302 1
Photographs by **József Hudetz**,
with the exception of Nos. 30, 33, 34, 43, 45, 58, 80, 98, 102,
107, 124, 126–129, 133 **(János Eifert)**; Nos. 104, 105, 108–111,
113–116, 118–122 **(Orsolya Ejury)**; No. 112 **(Károly Sáfrány)**

Design by **Erzsébet Szabados**

Printed in Hungary, 1987
Egyetemi Printing House, Budapest

Contents

I. The Origin of Hungarian Dog Breeds (Pál Sárkány) 7

    Hereditary Characteristics 8
    Judging the External Appearance of the Dog 9
    Breeding 13
    Rearing and Training Dogs 17
    Obedience Training 24

II. Hungarian Sheep Dogs (Imre Ócsag) 31

    A) Herding Sheep Dogs 31
        The Puli 31
        Standardization and Valuation of the Puli 33
        Judging the Appearance 34
        General Appearance 34
        Description of the Parts of the Body 35
        Characteristics for Evaluation 60
        Judging Pulis 75
        The Pumi 77
        The Pumi and its Changing Role during its History .. 79
        Standard Description 79
        Description of the Parts of the Body 80
        Judging Pumis 93
        The Mudi 94
        Standard Description 94
        Description of the Parts of the Body 95
        Judging Mudis 97
    B) Guarding Sheep Dogs 98
        The Kuvasz 98
        Origin 98
        Standard Description 100
        Description of the Parts of the Body 101
        Judging Kuvasz 118

The Komondor 120
Changes and Developments of the Komondor
in the Course of Time 137
Standard Description 138
Description of the Parts of the Body 139
Judging Komondors 151

III. Hungarian Hunting Dogs (Pál Sárkány) 153

The Hungarian Vizsla 153
The Hungarian Greyhound (Agár) 155
The Transylvanian Hound 156
The Standard of the Short-haired Hungarian Vizsla 157
General Features, Use 157
The Standard of the Short-haired Hungarian Vizsla 160
General Features, Use 160
The Standard of the Agár, the Hungarian Greyhound 194
General Features, Use 195
The Standard of the Transylvanian Hound 195
General Features, Use 195
About the Work Performed by Hunting Dogs 197
Basic Training 198
Training the Greyhound for Races 210
Coursing with Greyhounds 211
Hunting with Hounds 212
Bibliography 214

I. THE ORIGIN OF HUNGARIAN DOG BREEDS

There is relatively little documentation about the origin of Hungarian dog breeds, so we have to rely mainly on logical deduction when trying to trace their evolution.

It seems likely that the majority of the nine native recognized and registered breeds arrived in the Carpathian Basin during the Great Migration preceding the Magyars, the Huns and Avars, then with the Magyars and later on with the immigrating Pechenegs and Cumanians as their sheep dogs and hunting dogs.

All over the world, many scholars undertake scientific studies regarding the origin of Hungarian dog breeds. The present state of research permits only a supposition, namely, that these breeds were at home on the grass-grown steppes of Asia and were brought to their present home by the Magyars during the Great Migration.

The strong hereditary traits by which these breeds preserved their characteristics was a great help to researchers, enabling comparative examinations to verify theories concerning a period of over 1,000 years.

According to some scientific viewpoints the prototypes of the dog first appeared about 40 million years ago, in the transition period between the Eocene and the Miocene, when the *Myacis,* a carnivorous mammal appeared, now regarded as the joint ancestor of the bear and the dog.

It is not our intention to go into details on the evolution history of the dog, but we must underline the fact that dogs, as the very first domesticated animals, were the companion of man from ancient times.

A high degree of adaptation is characteristic of the dog. There is no other species of animal on earth represented in such variety. At present there are over 400 varieties in evidence, about 300 of these have officially accepted and internationally recorded "breed standard" descriptions with the Fédération Cynologique Internationale (FCI), the World Cynological Organization, which also records nine Hungarian breeds. These are: the Puli, the Pumi, the Mudi (the smaller sheep and cattle dogs); the Komondor and the Kuvasz (the large sheep and cattle dogs); the short-haired and the wire-haired Vizsla, the Hungarian Greyhound and the Transylvanian Hound.

Hereditary Characteristics

All Hungarian dog breeds, especially the shepherd dogs, have an excellent genetic transmission.

The selective breeding of Hungarian dogs was begun in the second half of the 19th century, the instigator being István Széchenyi.*

Valued features and properties of the dogs were developed in the course of many centuries of selective breeding. Shepherds travelled long distances to have their bitches mated by worthy dogs. In general the value of a good sheep dog equalled that of an adult sheep or cow. Breeding of hunting dogs was undertaken with similar care though the science of genetics was practically unknown.

Eliminating faults through careful choice of mate has been understood for many centuries. It was well known, for instance, that a dipping back cannot be improved by using a roach-backed partner, as this would result in even more exaggeration in the offspring.

We know that the carriers of heredity are chromosomes and DNA. The traits of puppies are genetically stabilized by way of cell division. It is not yet known whether the bitch or the male dog has the dominant role in heredity; opinions differ, but there is no scientific corroboration for either.

It is erroneous to believe that heredity is sex-linked. The pups manifest either the traits of the dam or of the sire. It is because some of the traits of one parent develop in a dominant way while those of the other are recessive. Recessive traits may nevertheless become dominant again in the following or in a later generation.

On heredity the point to remember is that it is disposition to some trait that is inherited. It then depends on the environment how this disposition develops. Acquired habits and features, on the other hand, cannot be inherited.

Although these are scientifically proved facts, the dispute concerning heredity of acquired traits still goes on. Certain people mention the hereditary ability of sheep dogs in guarding or rounding up the flock or the nose of gun dogs, to prove their point. It should be remembered that in both cases we are faced with acquired traits that had been genetically fixed in the course of centuries, even millennia. Such traits are passed on to the pups by way of chromosomes and not through the environment. In the same way amputation and artificial injuries cannot be inherited, as for instance the docked tail of Hungarian Vizslas, though docking has been practised for a number of generations. Occasionally new characteristics may appear in a species but these were brought about through

---

* Count István Széchenyi (1791–1860), statesman and political writer, was one of the most important figures of the Hungarian Reform Movement. He was the founder of the Hungarian Academy of Sciences, instigator of river control in Hungary. It was at Széchenyi's initiative that the first permanent bridge (Chain Bridge) was constructed between Pest and Buda. He also established controlled horse breeding and horse racing in Hungary.

spontaneous mutation or some other mode influencing heredity and are then fixed genetically.

No genetic fixation is possible of traits acquired through training, and they cannot be inherited either. Here again it is the instinct that is inherited which can be further improved through environmental influence or, in the lack of it, when this instinct does not manifest itself. Thus with the offspring of an excellent gun dog we can but hope for these traits to appear.

The science of genetics also studies the problem of inheriting intelligence. The manifold abilities of Hungarian dog breeds, their often amazing intelligence is an excellent basis for studying scientific hypotheses. The ability to inherit intelligence is less easy to assess than the transmission of coat colour. Colours can be graded while the manifestation of intelligence is influenced by many factors. Also, there is no objective standard to decide how much had been inherited and how much acquired from the behaviour and intelligence of a dog. However, the wide range of intelligence observed among different breeds indicates that intelligence may have a genetic foundation.

Judging the External Appearance of the Dog

It is well known to dog breeders that exterior characteristics go hand in hand with a dog's capabilities. This connection may be a positive or a negative one. In judging the exterior of a dog we gain clues to the abilities we cannot see. When judging Hungarian sheep dogs and gun dogs the emphasis is on the breed standards, formulated to preserve working ability.

Individual judgement therefore compares the dog in question and the official standard.

General Rules of Judging

Dogs are judged posed and while moving. The dog must be observed from the front, the side and from behind, on smooth and level ground. The judge is advised to use a platform when judging the posed animal.

The judge employs two methods; one to analyse in detail each part of the body separately, and the other to assess the dog by the impression given of the whole outline.

From the front, we look first at the whole head, and then in detail at all the facial features, the teeth, the eyes and the ears. We then look at the chest, the shoulders, the front legs and the paws. From the side, it is the symmetry of the body, the relative proportion of trunk and limbs which we notice. We assess the angulation of the legs, the development of the muscle structure, and the set of ears and tail.

From behind we can judge the width of the back and the loins, we can see whether the dog is out at elbow, and we can appreciate the strength of the hindquarters. From this position we have also the best opportunity to judge the general condition of the dog.

Long-haired Hungarian breeds are rather difficult to judge because of the heavy coat.

Judging the Features

The head requires special attention because the breed characteristics can be best seen here. The head must reflect the sex of the animal and indicate its temperament, it must be of a size in proportion to the body. If the general impression of a head is not good it may be because the head is coarse or weak. It is said to be coarse when the bone structure is heavy and covered with thick tissue. Such a head is often part of a similar skeleton, on clumsy stolid animals. The head of a bitch is always more refined than that of a male. A coarse-headed bitch is said to have a masculine head. A head that has all the characteristics of the breed and is in good proportion to the body is called a noble head. A weak head is undesirable and is frequently accompanied by a too refined, degenerated physique. In case of male dogs it is called a "bitchy head".

From the profile the head is said to be long or short. It can have a well-defined or a rather flat stop. There are so-called ram-noses but also snipy muzzles. Both these traits are hereditary. Seen from above the head may be round, oval, square or wedge-shaped.

The ears may be well set, high set or low set. Regarding their shape they may be pricked ears, semi-erect, or pendent. They may be small, medium or big; their leather is said to be thick, fleshy or thin. The position of the ears and even more their mobility reflects watchfulness, temperament and the intelligence of a dog. E. g., ears laid back indicate that a dog means to attack, or conversely, is very pleased.

Eyes are said to be correct if their form, size, position and colour are characteristic of the breed and also they are in good proportion to the head. In all Hungarian breeds both protruding eyes and too deep-set small eyes are undesirable.

The lips of shepherd dogs should be tight and closed and should be well pigmented. In Vizslas somewhat looser flews are not a defect, though not liked. The teeth must be complete and regular. The teeth are indicated by their Latin names, thus I *(Incissivus)*, incisors, C *(Canicus)*, canine teeth, P *(Praemolaris)*, premolars, and M *(Molaris)*, molars. Numbering the teeth starts from the incisors, to the right and the left, backwards through the premolars and molars.

The Arabic numerals beside the Latin initials indicate the ordinal number. When examining *the teeth* we also judge the bite which is correct if it is a scissors bite, while, an overshot or undershot bite is not permitted.

When judging *the neck and nape,* we mention the angle of junction, the shape and the length which all have to be in accordance with the breed. Thus, while in shepherd dogs a long neck is regarded as a fault, it is permitted in Vizslas and required in Greyhounds. If the neck is not sufficiently muscular it is called a weak neck while the contrary, a short and throughout thick neck, is called a stuffy neck. (Both are defects.)

When judging *the body,* the muscularity and height of the withers are an important aspect. Short and loaded withers give a roachback-look, while an unsufficiently muscular back shows sharp withers. If the spine is sunken between the shoulder blades, we speak of sagging withers. Sagging withers and loose shoulders are seen in young animals best, by giving them sufficient exercise to develop their muscles.

The spine is judged with the back, the loins and the hindquarter. Special attention is paid here to the line of the back, the loins and to the length of the back. The back should be straight and firm. Defective is a saddle back (sagging in behind the shoulders), but its reverse, a carp or roachback cannot be tolerated either with Hungarian breeds. A tough, well-sprung dog has short, wide and muscular loins. Long, so-called serpent loins (mostly also narrow and poorly muscled) is the sign of a weak constitution. The last third of the body is the croup consisting of the sacrum, the hip bone, and the first tail vertebrae. The croup is said to be regular if it is proportionately long and wide, muscular, and slopes gently from the sacrum towards the pelvis and the upper thighs. A flat croup or an overgrown one (the height of which exceeds that of the withers) is defective. The latter, however, is tolerated in young animals.

The carriage of *the tail,* its setting, its length, curve and hairiness are all important aspects when judging the characteristic features of the breed. A defect is a too high-set or low-set tail, often accompanied by defective hindquarters. Thus, for instance a low-set tail derives from a sloping croup.

The rib-cage should be deep and the ribs well-sprung. Such chests indicate well-developed lungs and give plenty of heart room. A shallow chest is undesirable. Besides the width and the depth of the rib-cage its length is also of importance. Thus a short and too broad chest results in an unpleasant "lion's chest". If the rib-cage is flat and narrow behind the shoulder blades and the elbows, we speak about a lack of heart room, which is regarded as a defect.

Seen from the front, *the brisket* should be broad and the shoulders well developed and muscular. A narrow brisket and a "pigeon's chest" is a defect.

The abdomen should be round and in direct continuation of the chest. An exception to this rule is the well tucked up belly of Greyhounds' and in case of Vizslas, the slightly tucked up flanks. A sagging belly is defective, though it is tolerated in bitches that have had several litters.

The feet should be judged as well from the front, as from the back and from the side. Seen from the front and from the back the feet should be parallel to each other. If they deviate inwards, this results in a narrow posture, while if they turn outwards, this gives a too wide posture. If the hocks converge we call them cow-hockedness, while if they bend outwards, the dog has bow-legs. Splay feet show outward turned paws. Seen from the side the posture of the forelimbs is correct if they stand perpendicularly from the elbow joint down to the wrist, while the pasterns (the metatarsus) stand—depending on the breed—at an angle of 45 to 80 degrees to the ground.

The posture of the hind legs is correct if seen from the side, a perpendicular line drawn from the edge of the hip joint touches the hocks. Steep stifles resulting in too straight legs are equally faulty as are sabre-legs, i.e., when the skin-bone and the metatarsus enclose only an angle of 135 degrees or less.

When examining *the genitals* the requirement is that they be healthy and complete. Testicles are always to be examined as cryptorchism is hereditary and such animals must be excluded from breeding.

Determining the Age of Dogs

Determining the age of a dog, though not a specific aspect of judging, is still indispensable for a breeder. With the change of age, we speak about puppies (till 6 months), saplings (yearlings), and full-grown animals.

Determining the age is done on the basis of the animal's teeth, which show the age with approximate accuracy from the appearance of the milk teeth, through the shedding of teeth, to the wearing off of the permanent ones. But when judging the wear of teeth the kind of food the dog receives has to be considered as well, because if the dog receives a lot of bones it is obvious that the teeth wear down sooner than if the animal is fed pulpy food. Regarding age, teeth give us the following information:

At birth, the teeth are not visible.

At the age of 1 month: the four milk canines appear.

At the age of 1 to 1 ½ months: the milk incisors and premolars erupt.

Between the age of 2 and 5 months: the permanent incisors appear instead of the milk incisors.

At the age of 5 months: the permanent premolars replace the milk premolars.

At the age of 6 months: the permanent canines replace the milk canines.

At the age of 1 year: all incisors have 3 prongs.

At the age of 2 years: the highest cusps, generally the middle ones of the incisors, are worn off.

At the age of 3 years: all the cusps begin to wear off.

At the age of 4 to 5 years: the cusps of all the incisors are worn flat.

At the age of 6 to 9 years: the whole crown of the incisors starts to wear off.

Age can also be guessed from the change in the proportions of the body. For instance, the head and the extremities of a young dog are proportionally bigger to the trunk. An overgrown croup is also a frequent phenomenon in young dogs. Such disproportions disappear with age. Also changes in the coat can be observed with the change in age. Around its eighth year, a dog generally begins to go gray around the muzzle, the eyes and the eyebrows. It loses its former liveliness, its gait becomes slow. The teeth start falling out and even the bark changes. We sometimes hear about dogs that attained the age of 20 to 25 years. This however, is very rare.

Breeding

The great variety of the species "dog" is also manifested in the case of Hungarian breeds. The three small shepherd dogs: the Puli, the Pumi and the Mudi, were bred basically for the same purpose. This is true also of the two big kinds, the Kuvasz and the Komondor and, among gun dogs, the two kinds of Vizslas. All over the world dogs bred for the same purpose show an even higher variety than is the case with Hungarian breeds. Both small and big shepherd dogs as well as different gun dogs can be found in dozens of varieties and breeds. The pioneers of Hungarian shepherd dog breeding were Géza Buzzi, Károly Monostori and Emil Raitsits, who—on the principle of mass-selection breeding—selected the individuals which best represented the breed and then carried out continuous planned breeding and propagation.

For the practical breeder there are three possibilities. The first and most natural is selection on basis of appearance (phenotype), i.e., by visual judgement. The other way is selection on the basis of origin. Here the pedigree is most helpful as the prices obtained at dog-shows and other measures of value give responsible information regarding the potential quality of the progeny. The third possibility is selection for breeding on the basis of the quality of the progeny. The latter is also called brood examination. It is also the safest and most expedient method determining the genetic properties of the individual. As a new generation of dogs is born in 2 to 2½ years and the selected animals can be kept in breeding for 5 times this time, it requires a relatively short time to see the value of the descendants, thus determining the important genetic quality of the parents. This method also has the advantage that with a dog found to be excellent this way, line-breeding or inbreeding is possible within one life-span.

Dogs are sufficiently prolific so that while still in breeding a selection on the basis of the descendants' quality and thus improvement of the breed is possible. For good results, only patience and steadfastness is needed, besides some knowledge, of course. Dogs found to be good transmitters of their qualities are of the highest value. It may happen that a dog coming of excellent ancestors, completely conforming to standard specifications, cannot transmit its traits and qualities to its descendants and is therefore of little value for breeding purposes.

The mode of breeding applied should be chosen according to our experience. If our knowledge is small the most expedient way is to start breeding with pedigreed, pure-bred animals and to leave any other method (introduction of new blood with related animals, inbreeding and different cross-breeding modes) to breeders with long experience and knowledge who know the stock, and who have but one aim: the improvement of a breed.

Mating

Selecting the right mate for our bitch is a responsible task. On it depends the result of breeding. The intention is that both the male and the bitch be, as far as possible, of similar appearance, character, and of similar quality. Males are always to be judged more severely than bitches, as a male can have more descendants.

Selecting the suitable sire should not be carried out on the basis of pedigree alone. A more thorough knowledge is always needed and we should decide only after having compared all aspects of our choice.

In selecting the male certain basic principles should be remembered.

a) No constitutional defect can be ameliorated with an opposite extreme. Thus, a sagging back mated with an arched back will never result in a straight back.

b) Very young or elderly animals should be mated with ones in the prime of their life. It is not expedient to mate a young bitch with an old dog.

c) When we want to mate our bitch, it is wise to select two males, as it may easily happen that one gets suddenly ill, has met with an accident, or, quite simply, that the bitch does not accept our choice.

Pregnancy

After finding the suitable partner, the dogs can be mated. Knowing that with dogs pregnancy lasts 9 weeks or 63 days, we can now easily calculate the day of whelping, though deviations of 3 to 4 days or even a week are possible. The pregnancy calendar hereunder is a good aid.

In the early days of pregnancy the bitch does not require any special treatment, the usual food and care is sufficient. However, around 3 to 4 weeks after mating, the bitch starts to be finicky. From now on she requires a good mixed diet, with emphasis on extra protein and a balanced vitamin/mineral supplement. From the second half of pregnancy the bitch should not be forced to do strenuous exercise, but on the other hand, she should not be pampered but kept

Pregnancy Calendar

	Days
Mating: January	1 2 3 4 5 6 7 8 9 10 11 12 13 14 15 16 17 18 19 20 21 22 23 24 25 26 27 28 29 30 31
Whelping: March	5 6 7 8 9 10 11 12 13 14 15 16 17 18 19 20 21 22 23 24 25 26 27 28 29 30 31 1 2 3 4
Mating: February	1 2 3 4 5 6 7 8 9 10 11 12 13 14 15 16 17 18 19 20 21 22 23 24 25 26 27 28
Whelping: April	5 6 7 8 9 10 11 12 13 14 15 16 17 18 19 20 21 22 23 24 25 26 27 28 29 30 1 2
Mating: March	1 2 3 4 5 6 7 8 9 10 11 12 13 14 15 16 17 18 19 20 21 22 23 24 25 26 27 28 29 30 31
Whelping: May	3 4 5 6 7 8 9 10 11 12 13 14 15 16 17 18 19 20 21 22 23 24 25 26 27 28 29 30 1 2
Mating: April	1 2 3 4 5 6 7 8 9 10 11 12 13 14 15 16 17 18 19 20 21 22 23 24 25 26 27 28 29 30
Whelping: June	3 4 5 6 7 8 9 10 11 12 13 14 15 16 17 18 19 20 21 22 23 24 25 26 27 28 29 30 1 2
Mating: May	1 2 3 4 5 6 7 8 9 10 11 12 13 14 15 16 17 18 19 20 21 22 23 24 25 26 27 28 29 30 31
Whelping: July	3 4 5 6 7 8 9 10 11 12 13 14 15 16 17 18 19 20 21 22 23 24 25 26 27 28 29 30 31 1 2
Mating: June	1 2 3 4 5 6 7 8 9 10 11 12 13 14 15 16 17 18 19 20 21 22 23 24 25 26 27 28 29 30
Whelping: August	3 4 5 6 7 8 9 10 11 12 13 14 15 16 17 18 19 20 21 22 23 24 25 26 27 28 29 30 31 1
Mating: July	1 2 3 4 5 6 7 8 9 10 11 12 13 14 15 16 17 18 19 20 21 22 23 24 25 26 27 28 29 30 31
Whelping: September	2 3 4 5 6 7 8 9 10 11 12 13 14 15 16 17 18 19 20 21 22 23 24 25 26 27 28 29 30 1 2
Mating: August	1 2 3 4 5 6 7 8 9 10 11 12 13 14 15 16 17 18 19 20 21 22 23 24 25 26 27 28 29 30 31
Whelping: October	3 4 5 6 7 8 9 10 11 12 13 14 15 16 17 18 19 20 21 22 23 24 25 26 27 28 29 30 31 1 2
Mating: September	1 2 3 4 5 6 7 8 9 10 11 12 13 14 15 16 17 18 19 20 21 22 23 24 25 26 27 28 29 30
Whelping: November	3 4 5 6 7 8 9 10 11 12 13 14 15 16 17 18 19 20 21 22 23 24 25 26 27 28 29 30 1 2
Mating: October	1 2 3 4 5 6 7 8 9 10 11 12 13 14 15 16 17 18 19 20 21 22 23 24 25 26 27 28 29 30 31
Whelping: December	3 4 5 6 7 8 9 10 11 12 13 14 15 16 17 18 19 20 21 22 23 24 25 26 27 28 29 30 31 1 2
Mating: November	1 2 3 4 5 6 7 8 9 10 11 12 13 14 15 16 17 18 19 20 21 22 23 24 25 26 27 28 29 30
Whelping: January	3 4 5 6 7 8 9 10 11 12 13 14 15 16 17 18 19 20 21 22 23 24 25 26 27 28 29 30 31 1
Mating: December	1 2 3 4 5 6 7 8 9 10 11 12 13 14 15 16 17 18 19 20 21 22 23 24 25 26 27 28 29 30
Whelping: February	2 3 4 5 6 7 8 9 10 11 12 13 14 15 16 17 18 19 20 21 22 23 24 25 26 27 28 1 2 3

in natural circumstances, with sufficient sunlight, exercise in fresh air, and plenty but not too much food. The bitch should not be given very cold water to drink and should not have access to putrid food.

In the weeks preceding the whelping the bitch will prepare a bed in which to give birth to her young. Give her maximum help, ensuring a quiet corner, where in a suitable size box the difficult process of giving birth is possible and where, afterwards, the animal can have some peace and seclusion.

In the first half of pregnancy the bitches' figure does not change. Pregnancy can be visually observed only after 30 days. Two weeks before whelping the nipples will start to swell, because milk secretion has begun.

The whelping box should be prepared with special care. Line the box with straw or shavings, and make the sides high enough to contain the puppies.

Whelping

When the time of throwing approaches, the bitch becomes more and more restless, so we better keep an eye on her, although usually no human interference is required in a normal whelping. After the escape of the amniotic fluid the puppies appearing in the birth canal are born without special help on our part. The bitch severs the umbilical cord of all the whelps with her teeth, eats the foetal membrane and licks all the young dry. The bitch should then be given fresh but not cold milk or at least fresh water.

Generally small dogs have a litter of two, three or four, while big ones ten to twelve or even more.

If any delay or obstruction is observed during the whelping or if the bitch does not go into labour when expected, the help of a veterinary surgeon should be sought. In this way potential complications can be avoided, and it may be the only way to guarantee the health of both mother and litter.

When whelping is complete, the bitch should be taken for a short walk so that the whelping box may be cleaned by a helper.

From the first litter not more than three or four, from the later ones six whelps can be kept. Those seeming the most suitable for further breeding purposes should be selected when having their first checking directly after their birth. More than the above number of whelps should be reared with the aid of a foster mother.

Suckling

The whelps, immediately on being born, crowd under their mother in search of food. A well-fed bitch generally has the necessary amount of milk. Her milk secretion starts one or two days before the pups really need it. For the new-born puppies, the composition of the early milk is of special interest in the first days of their life as this milk removes the meconium (the first bowel movement), and also contains protective anti-bodies.

In case of need, and depending on the number of whelps, the mother's milk production can be increased by adding hormone preparations, vitamins and minerals to her food. Milk secretion is an intensive physiological process, the bitch is apt to ensure the milk necessary for the whelps even by endangering her own system. Therefore, she must be fed well so as not to lose weight and to produce rich and abundant milk for the development of the bone structure of her young.

Suitable husbandry with adequate exercise also helps milk secretion. For this reason, the whelps should not be left with the mother all day, but, beginning from the second day after whelping, the bitch should be taken for walks regularly, without, of course, overdoing it.

The milk secretion of the front mammary glands is less than that of the back ones. Therefore, the smaller whelps should be placed on the back teats while feeding. With this little extra care the litter will be even within a short time.

Weaning

The whelps are born blind, deaf and without teeth. Their eyes open when they are two weeks old, and soon they start to hear. Accordingly they have to be accustomed gently to light and sound. In the first two weeks of their life their excreta cause no trouble as it is cleared up by the mother. Later, however, it is our task to begin house-training. From the third week the pups may be offered milk thickened with a fine grade of cereal, to accustom them to solid food.

Weaning should be started gradually from the 6th week on. In the first 3 weeks the whelps should be fed on demand by the dam 5–6 times daily. Later, by separating the bitch from her young, suckling should be reduced gradually and replaced with other food. But even after the whelps are completely weaned, they should be left with the mother at least till they are 7 to 8 weeks old, as she can teach them a number of things. A practised breeder can by then already select the most promising ones.

Rearing and Training Dogs

Due to rapid urbanization, there are less and less dogs living in a natural environment. The immense meadows were broken up and used for plant cultivation; modern animal husbandry breeds in stables. Thus, together with people, more and more dogs are found in towns where, first of all, dogs kept in flats live in the least natural environment. By the presence of dogs, man tries to conjure around himself the natural environment he misses so much.

Though the number of shepherds is decreasing owing to mechanization, the demand for shepherd dogs has not diminished at all. They become faithful companions even if forced to live in towns.

The great interest in Hungarian shepherd dogs, both abroad and in Hungary, indicates their popularity. Their loveable nature endears them to city-dwellers and makes them faithful companions.

Though shepherd dogs lived in the open for centuries they easily adapted to live indoors and quickly got used to the changed environment and circumstances. However, we should try to establish conditions which could suitably substitute for nature that the dog misses so much.

The mode of life of watch dogs is much more true to nature than of those living in apartments. An apartment seems comfortable to humans, the dog, however, does not require it, only gets accustomed and comes to accept it. Dogs kept in apartments are generally rather restricted in movement as their master has often but very little time to walk them. Also, their food is sometimes rather one-sided. As unsuitable keeping and care causes less pleasure than worry and difficulties to the dog owners, we will go into more detail on this problem.

Accommodation

Whether a dog is kept in the house or around the house, it is necessary that it have a place for itself. In a house with a garden, a well-constructed kennel gives sufficient protection, even in winter. All Hungarian breeds are accustomed to cold winters, even the short-haired ones. A kennel should preferably have a removable roof, so it can be kept clean without difficulty. It is best built from wood, as timber is a good insulator. The floor of the hut should not be right on the ground, but should stand on socles or bricks. It should be lined with straw, hay, moss or shavings, changed at least every fortnight.

It is best to fence a part of the garden where the dog can be free with access to the kennel. The kennel should be situated so that the run gets the sunshine, and the door should not be in the direction of the prevailing wind.

For dogs kept in apartments, it is equally a major requirement that they have their permanent and very own place. Beginning from puppy-age, the dog should get accustomed to it and taught to leave it only on permission. If it has the run of the apartment, it will cause nuisance both to itself and to people. The owner can save himself a lot of trouble if he keeps these rules and makes his dog keep them.

The place of a dog in an apartment should be a secluded spot or corner, never in front of a door, because we may stumble over the dog and also because of draught, harmful to both humans and animals. The dog's place should not be near to a radiator or the fire. Too much warmth causes discomfort especially to long-haired shepherd dogs which stand the vicissitudes of winter much better than the warmth of radiators.

Suitable beds for dogs are dog baskets, a shallow box or even a folded blanket. Old, worn clothes should not serve as blanket. They are uncomfortable for the animal and are difficult to keep clean.

All Hungarian breeds accommodate to city life very quickly and quickly become an integral part of the life of their owner, but still, they do require constant care (regular walks, good food). If the dog is accustomed to a certain time for his walks, there will be no problems regarding defecation and urination. If the dog is taken for a walk three times a day, it is best to arrange that the walks be shortly after his meals, and that the last walk be as late as possible.

All Hungarian breeds, shepherd and gun dogs alike, are basically friendly, loyal, and eager to learn. If suitably trained, they give much pleasure in ownership. It is a basic rule that the master himself should train the dog, or somebody the dog likes and accepts. One should never start teaching and training in an irritable mood, as dogs intuitively feel and react to human moods.

The care of the coat of long-haired shepherd dogs is especially important in a flat. Vizslas and Hungarian Greyhounds, though they require a lot of exercise, proved to be excellent city-companions.

A New Dog in the Home

If possible, the dog should be acquired when still a puppy. Let it get introduced thoroughly to the new environment. Members of the family should not frighten it with too much love, and rough treatment should be avoided, as it may well be reflected in the dog's behaviour later on.

A young dog can be best accustomed to its environment with praise, and not by punishment. If, for instance, the dog willingly goes to its bed, it should be praised and given a small tit-bit. It should never be chastised in its own place, which should always mean security for the animal.

House-training is the most crucial task for both the owner and the puppy. It should last no longer than two to three weeks, but if it is carried out consistently, it may be done in a few days. The first and main step is to take the dog out of doors and stay with it there until it has relieved itself. The moment this happens, the animal should be praised and patted. If the puppy makes a mistake indoors, the animal should be scolded but never rub its nose into its excreta. If we notice that the dog is preparing to relieve itself, it should be immediately taken outdoors and kept there until it performs. This should be repeated again and again, with lots of patience, until the dog understands what we want from him.

Eating starts the peptic glands to work and this induces the dog to discharge.

It is therefore advisable to take the dog outdoors soon after feeding. Sometimes a dog will show its intention of relieving itself by either barking or scratching at the door. After five o'clock in the evening, the dog should receive neither food nor water, if possible. Before going to bed, we should take it outdoors once more to relieve itself and in the morning, immediately after waking, the young dog should again be taken outdoors.

To get the puppy accustomed to its name, it should be called repeatedly by name, and be patted and praised. This way it will answer to its name quickly.

The Collar and Leash

Collar and leash are compulsory both in the country and in town, so the dog has to get accustomed to them at an early age. In the beginning the dog may of course show some aversion; later on, however, it will be happy when it sees the leash taken up, as it means walking outdoors. It may be advisable to put an elastic collar on the puppy in the very beginning to accustom it to wearing a collar.

Bad Habits in the Flat

When a dog jumps up at people, this causes embarrassment both to its master and to the guests of the house. There are several methods to discourage the dog. The most suitable is to hit it lightly with a rolled-up newspaper, causing no pain but making a loud noise. At the same time, tell the dog in a cross voice that it did something bad. Another bad habit is licking and chewing everything, which should be discouraged from the earliest age. It is suggested to smear favourite spots with vinegar, tobacco powder or some other agent with an intensive smell or disagreeable taste.

Dogs love to sit in armchairs, on couches and any other soft furniture, even if they have their own comfortable place. Usually, dogs crawl on furniture in the absence of the master in search of his scent, but it is advisable to discourage them while very young. If we do not forbid this habit immediately, it will cause the ruin of our furniture.

Feeding

The food requirements of a dog depend on its size and the work demanded from it. It depends quantitatively on the size but is independent, regarding its composition. As any living organism, dogs require five basic nutrients: protein, fat, carbohydrate, minerals and vitamins. Proteins are contained in meat, meat meal, fishmeal, milk, eggs, mill-cakes, etc. Fats can be both animal fats and vegetable oils, while carbohydrates are to be found in bread and cereals. All living organisms also need minerals, primarily calcium, phosphorus, and salt. Vitamins are just as necessary additive nutrients for the animal organism as for man.

The dog's diet has to be worked out according to its needs. When strenuous muscular work is demanded from the dog—racing or working—a high protein diet is needed, but too much of carbohydrates will cause obesity. Young animals need more protein than adults, as they have to build up their muscular frame.

None of the Hungarian breeds has special dietary requirements. Like any dog, it is ready to "eat the best" but, if the quantity is sufficient, it may be fed quite plainly.

Up to the age of 12 months, dogs should be fed three times a day, the amount divided in 3 equal parts. When the animal is one year old, it is sufficient to feed it twice daily.

Meat should be given cut small, to prevent the dog from swallowing the lot without chewing. Fresh water should always be available. Always give the dog only the amount it eats with good appetite. If it does not eat the whole amount, the remainder should be put away and given—if not spoiled—at the next meal. If we have several dogs, each should have a separate dish. Dogs love bones. However, not every kind of bone is good for the dog. Poultry, rabbit, pig and lamb bones should not be fed as they splinter and may cause a perforation of the intestines during digestion. Most dogs like milk, but it is not wise to give too much, as it may cause digestive upsets.

All carbohydrates, including sugar, form an important energy source for dogs. Due to rapid oxidation, sugar is highly important for dogs from which strenuous work is required. Even so, gun dogs that are expected to run for long hours over difficult terrain very seldom get the amount of sugar of their calory requirement, while less active house-dogs are pampered with it. Sugar, together with other kinds of starch, is transformed into fat if not utilized for energy. This again causes obesity which is not only objectionable from an aesthetical point of view but is bad for the health causing indigestion, first of all. Dogs should never be given sugar before their main meal, because it will cause a loss of appetite. Let us keep in mind the human diet. It is not by chance that a meal always begins with an apéritif and finishes with a dessert or sweet wine. The sequence of dishes is related to the action of digestive juices.

Sheep dogs and also gun dogs are apt to eat putrid meat and carrion if they find it. But it is not advisable to let them have spoiled food as it may cause illness, even poisoning.

It is advisable to give the intended amount of food in one portion. Meat should be cut up and mixed with soup or vegetables to prevent the dog from gobbling its food. From time to time of course, meat can also be given separately, but always cut into rather small pieces.

A special problem is feeding sick dogs. If the animal runs a temperature, it is inactive and thus requires fewer calories. It should be given light food, soup, boiled (but not too warm) milk. Sick animals should receive relatively little to eat. If the dog suffers from indigestion, plain diet is advisable, if it is properly balanced nutritionally. Sick dogs should be given less fat and protein, and sugar should be withheld. Sick dogs should be taken to the veterinary surgeon who will also advise on their diet.

When feeding puppies, all of them should have separate dishes and should be given their food simultaneously, if possible. This prevents fights and ensures even portions. When eating from one dish, the puppies will gulp the food, being afraid of the others getting more. Also, the greedy ones will surely eat more than the less strong and less resourceful ones. In this way puppies with different temperaments will not give an evenly developed litter.

Before weaning, from 3 weeks old, the puppies should be given pulpy, milky food that is easily digested. After weaning they should be fed five times a day, then only four times, from 6 months to 12 months three times a day, and then only twice a day.

Young dogs should only be given as much as they eat up with a good appetite. Conditioned reflexes start the secretion of the dog's gastric juices when we begin preparing the food. Regularity is important in feeding so that the adjusted time reflex is not disturbed. When pups eat with reluctance, there must be something wrong with their digestion or else they are not active, happy dogs. By giving them a smaller amount, the appetite can be sharpened and they become better eaters. Water should be changed frequently to save it from getting warm or dirty.

Heavily seasoned food should not be fed; it is not good for the digestion. An exception to the rule is, of course, some salt mixed with the food.

Care should be taken to provide the pups with the necessary vitamins and mineral salts in the form of a measured dose of a balanced vitamin preparation, given in accordance with the manufacturer's instructions.

Puppies need bones not only for their calcium and to build a sound bone structure but also because they simply love to chew anything when young. Chewing is especially important when shedding their teeth. Big marrow bones are excellent as though the puppy is unable to eat them, their taste and smell induces the animal to chew them for long hours. Synthetic and imitation bones and chews are useful to exercise jaw muscles and also to while away the time. If nothing to chew is given to the puppy, it is apt to destroy household goods.

Bathing, Grooming

Neither Hungarian sheep dogs nor gun dogs require special grooming. Their coat is naturally beautiful but that does not mean that it ought to be ungroomed. Dogs living around or in the house should be clean and well groomed in the interest of the health of the owner and the family.

Grooming long coated shepherd dogs takes time, but the extra work required, if done regularly, is worth-while.

The coat of Vizslas and Greyhounds needs only brushing while that of the longer haired breeds, e.g. Kuvasz, Pumi and Mudi, needs combing, preferably with a metal comb. The coat of Pulis and Komondors should never be combed right out. Most grooming is needed around the hindquarters, where the hair is apt to become matted, but the aim is that coat should be corded here too. Never trim Hungarian breed dogs. If brushed regularly, or with short-haired types, if polished with silk cloth after brushing, their coat will always be beautifully shiny.

Feet need regular cleaning, especially in wet weather. Never permit your dog to enter the house with muddy paws, get him accustomed to having them cleaned. After a time the dog gets used to this and will wait to be cleaned before entering.

Ears should be examined frequently and excess wax should be removed so that hair and wax secretion may not cause obstruction in the auditory canal, leading to inflammation of the ear or even diminished hearing. Vizslas' ears are especially sensitive because they are pendulous and when retrieving in water or swimming, water easily enters the auditory canal. After bathing, dogs' ears should be dried carefully. Inflammation of the ear can be detected by the dog shaking its head or trying to scratch the ear with his foot or against a tree, a wall. In severe cases it is best to see the veterinary surgeon. Teeth should be examined monthly. If tartar is noticed, it should be removed by the vet as this may cause gingivitis and destroy tooth enamel leading to an early loss of the teeth. Some dogs do not like their ears or teeth examined, so it is best to do this from an early age.

On bathing there are differing opinions. Of course, bathing from time to time is part of grooming in general, especially in case of dogs kept indoors. Swimming in rivers does not make up for regular bathing, as rivers are sometimes polluted and muddy and also because after swimming dogs generally take a dust or sandbath, which makes them even more dirty.

None of the Hungarian breeds should be bathed until they are 6 months old. Frequent bathing should be avoided later on too. Even with dogs kept in an apartment, once a month is more than sufficient. It is best to bathe the dog under a shower, with hand-warm water. Use an oily shampoo, rinse carefully.

Both in winter and in summer, the animal should be thoroughly dried after its bath with rough towels. Do not let the dog loose after its bath, or it may well splash water all over the house. It is best to keep him covered with a big towel until completely dry.

After bathing, the dog's towels should be washed and the tub or basin disinfected. Nails should be attended to after the bath. If too long—because the dog does not walk enough—they may cause discomfort and should be cut. If the dog has sufficient exercise the nails wear down and cutting is not necessary.

Regular grooming involves cleaning the eyes and nose every day. For this purpose a clean soft cloth or damp cotton wool is best.

A dog's hygiene also requires a permanent lookout for external and internal parasites. If any, these should be immediately and carefully removed. All dogs need worming, whether working dogs or pets. Adults are usually wormed in the spring—your veterinary surgeon will supply the appropriate remedy. Bitches must also be wormed before mating.

Removing external parasites is just as important; not only dogs kept in the country but also those living in an apartment may attract fleas or lice. The dog indicates their presence by scratching or rolling about. Freeing the dog from such parasites causes no special worry, as suitable remedies can be had from the veterinarian.

We have already mentioned that Hungarian breeds are not delicate, requiring no special grooming. However, never forget that dogs living outdoors require care and grooming just as those living in an apartment.

Obedience Training

Dogs make agreeable companions if they are taught to behave in a cultured way, to carry out their allotted tasks without fail, and to be obedient. Any dog is suited to carry out a number of tasks. It is not some special breed characteristics we have in mind, but basic intelligence. The majority of dogs—and Hungarian ones without exception—have a high degree of intelligence. Of course each dog has its strong and its weak points which indicate some special line of training. For instance, small sheep dogs can be best trained to round up sheep or a herd, big ones to protect and guard while gun dogs will point, search, follow a trail and retrieve. These capabilities or inclinations are best judged individually as inclination and readiness does not only vary among humans but, because of their intelligence, also among dogs.

The scientific assessment of readiness and inclination is the task of dog-psychologists. In recent times, ethology and psychology have formed a more and more important part of research work connected with animals. Getting to know the ethology-psychology of domestic animals helps to develop their productivity. The same applies to dogs.

We know a number of excellent researchers working in the field of ethology-psychology, among them Professor Konrad Lorenz of the Ethology Chair at the Munich University, who has written a number of internationally known works treating dog-psychology.

Cyno-psychology, the science dealing with the nervous system of dogs, distinguishes four different temperaments: sanguinic (confident), choleric (bold), phlegmatic (placid) and sullen dogs. The order of the above distinction indicates also the degree of ability to learn. Sanguinic dogs are very often bright with a vivid but even temperament, intelligent, well-balanced. They can be trained easily, with lasting results, and are most suitable for any kind of work.

The term choleric means spirited, fiery, also unrestrained. Such dogs also can be trained well and with lasting results, but their training requires much more energy. These dogs react quickly to any stimulus but their inhibitions develop slowly.

The term placid covers dogs that are well-balanced, difficult to set on edge, but their equability is often akin to laziness. Their training requires a lot of patience and work, but they become reliable animals. They can be trained and used with good results for any type of work.

Sullen dogs are shy, unbalanced, their shyness is quite often coupled with slyness and untrustworthy behaviour. They cannot be trained with good results, their intelligence, due to their inhibitions, manifests itself with difficulty, and therefore they appear stubborn, mulish, even stupid.

These four main types of temperament are not sharply divided. One may safely say: no dog pertains to one category only, in the same way as there is no completely good or completely bad human being.

Methods of Training

The closer the dog lives to man, the more it becomes necessary that the animal obeys the wish of the master. This involves tasks pertaining to the so-called "basic training": walking on the leash, following its master without the use of a leash, and obeying such orders as: sit, come, down, stay, stand, go ahead, bark on command, to retrieve different objects, clear obstacles, etc. Special tasks are guarding-protecting as well as following a trail by scent. Training gun dogs is very specialized work.

Walking on a leash must be learned by every dog. The objective is that the dog stay beside its master, on a loose leash, whether he is standing, walking or running. The dog should always be on the left. When starting, a sound signal should be given, besides pulling gently at the leash. Should the animal lag behind or try to run, pulling at the leash should be used to accustom it to keep close to its master, giving at the same time the "heel" command. After pulling at the leash, it should be loosened immediately, enabling the dog to walk by the owner's side. The leash should not be pulled again until the dog repeatedly tries to lag behind or run. If the dog fulfilled the command, it should be patted and praised. It is best to practise beside a wall or a fence where the dog has no possibility to dodge away. Never forget to praise and pat your dog when he returns to heel.

The next disciplinary task is to make the dog walk at heel without a leash. This can be practised when walking on a loose leash is already carried out without fault. Once again, the dog should be praised whenever he carries out this task well.

One of the very first and most often applied disciplinary operations is to "sit" because a number of other training exercises are based on it. Therefore, to sit has to be taught very thoroughly, so that dog never moves away from a sitting position until given another command by his master. "Sit" is taught by gently tugging at the leash (upwards) and at the same time guiding the dog's rear end down to a sitting position. The moment he sits, the dog should be praised. When practising "sit", the word "sit" should be repeated loudly.

Sitting as a corrective exercise is very suitable increasing the dog's obedience. When in a sitting position, the distance between dog and man should be increased gradually, looking back from time to time and repeating the commands "sit" and "stay". As mentioned, the distance should be increased gradually, and, as in the case of any other training exercise, praise should follow good work.

Teaching the dog to "come" is another important step in training. A well-trained dog is expected to return to his master when called or given a signal to come to heel and sit at the master's left side. "Come" as an obedience exercise gives pleasure to the dog as it is then permitted to return to its master where it feels in security, but this is also a pleasure to the owner. This movement can be taught by commanding "come here" or "to me", by a signal made with the arm or with a whistle.

The next step is "down". Though the most natural position for a dog is to lie, it has still to be taught, as there is a difference between resting and lying down on command. In case of guard dogs, "down" is practised through the command "down", in case of gun dogs by raising the rifle to shoot.

If "down" is not learned easily by the dog, one should step on the leash and thus force the dog to lay its head on the ground, while repeating the command "down" and, of course, praising the animal when "down" is carried out well.

The next phase of training after "down" is to get the dog to get up again. This exercise consists of two parts depending on whether the dog is wanted to stand up from a "down" position or given the command "stop" while walking or running.

If a sitting or lying dog is made to stand up and does not obey the command, gently put your foot under his belly, lift him in this way while repeating the command and praising the animal. The dog can also be induced to stand by gently tugging the leash upwards and by simulating starting. This means stepping out but not moving an inch and tugging at the leash at the same time. These exercises and the repeated command will bring good results.

A more difficult process is to accustom the dog to "stay", which can be taught very gradually and through steadfastness, since, as the dog loves its master, it immediately wants to follow him the moment he moves.

"Stay" in a standing position has to be started by "stay" in a sitting one. The dog is at the "sit" in front of us and the command "stay" is given while also pointing to the spot where it has to remain. When obeying the command, the dog should be praised and patted. Whether sitting or standing, the dog has to endure his master moving off a shorter or longer distance and to stay until the command releasing him.

The next phase of training is to send the dog "forward". This means different things to different breeds. When sending shepherd dogs forward, this is with the aim of herding up the flock, while with gun dogs it is to flush out or retrieve game, but when training guard dogs, sending forward is related to quite special tasks. When training the dog to go "forward" a number of different methods are used or are combined. The fact that the dog is playful can be utilized excellently when exercising, as the dog running about without a leash can be sent along by raising our arm and commanding "forward". The animal will fulfil this task even more willingly if we run with him, a few steps at least. After a certain distance the dog should be called to stop and recalled to heel. Of course praise is due to the dog when carrying out the command.

Sending the dog forward should not be practised after taking off the leash, but only after the animal has fulfilled successfully "heeling" without the leash. If these two exercises are mixed up, the dog will start to run away any time the leash has been taken off.

A dog sent forward should be recalled after some time elapses, because if called back immediately, he will be bewildered and this hinders the process of reflex action.

With gun dogs, sending forward means hunting out and pointing the game, i.e. the beginning of a specific work-phase. The command for sending forward the dog is "forward", "search" and the dog has to work all by himself, looking back at his master from time to time. He has to go over the ground, whether it be coppice, reed bank or stubble higher than he himself. He has to point the game to the hunter by standing rigidly and "putting a spell" in the game.

Dogs have to be taught to make a sound, that is, to bark. The difference between spontaneous barking and barking at a command is that while in the former case the dog is the initiator, in the latter it is the master.

Many people teach their dog to bark not only by commanding "bark" but also with the word "greet", particularly dogs kept in an apartment. Thus the animal greets the guest with a sound he has been permitted to emit and resists the habit of yapping.

Dogs can be taught to bark in a disciplined way before their daily meal and, of course, before their usual time of walk. Dogs can hardly wait for the moment when they are taken for a walk and in many cases, when one just touches the leash, they jump about, yelping.

In the same way dogs kept in kennels or in a box are also happy to see their master. Teaching the dog to bark when permitted can solve the problem of undisciplined, unwanted barking.

Retrieving, that is, bringing back objects can be taught to any breed but it is primarily the task of guard and gun dogs. A dog in a playful mood will quickly learn to retrieve a dumbbell, a piece of wood or a ball used for retrieving purposes and will bring it back willingly. Disciplining the animal has to be begun at this moment, as the dog has to give his master the retrieved object in a sitting position, and not, as it often happens, by running round the master, calling him to play.

An integral and important task of gun dogs is to retrieve without fail. This is especially difficult when the dog has to find and retrieve shot game from a thicket, reed or, in winter, from ice-cold water. For such work dogs should be generously praised.

Dogs have also to be taught to surmount obstacles, to clear a fence or a bush. The dog has to be accustomed gradually to such tasks.

Training Sheep Dogs

An organized, standard method of training sheep dogs has never been recorded. Shepherds always used dogs trained by themselves and these dogs learned the rudimentary knowledge from their mothers. This training was then continued by the shepherd. Good shepherd dogs are enthusiastic at rounding up and are also the absolute masters of the flock, being held in awe by the animals they guard. This hereditary rounding-up instinct was utilized many centuries ago; possibly at the very beginning of domestication it was on this basis that shepherd dogs were selected. With their help nomadic people drove their herds across the country and for this purpose they are still used for instance in the North with reindeer. When selecting sheep dogs not only their looks but their usefulness and working ability have to be considered. These features can be seen with certainty only at the age of 3 to 4 months, though sometimes even 6-week old puppies reveal their herding capabilities.

There are tests which may aid in selection; some behaviour patterns of the puppies can be useful indications. Such empirical signs are, for instance, behaviour while eating. If a puppy can be pushed away from the dish by another, it will never make a good shepherd dog. A bunch of keys dropped near the dog causes a reaction. Stability can be tested by suddenly opening an umbrella. Also the dog's behaviour with a stranger tells us something about its character. Does it start to play or avoid the visitor, or does it show aggression? These are all signs which help us to draw conclusions on the animal's character. Barking, for instance, is not always a welcome manifestation, as dogs very often also bark when afraid.

The basis of successful training is that the dog is devoted to its master. It is of major importance that the dog is willing to please man and that praise, after a successful exercise, gives it pleasure.

To give orders, words and signs are used that the dog will come to understand after continuous practice. The emphasis is of more importance than the meaning as it will be kept in mind by the dog and will cause the development of conditional reflexes. The reflex brought about on a basis of systematic repetition can be fixed without difficulty. Teaching and practice compound to train the dog in good habits. Without these, dog's shepherding instinct may develop in a wrong direction and it will round up the herd even if not needed, or, what is worse, may demonstrate its rounding-up instinct with the poultry of our neighbour.

As with other dogs, working sheep dogs should have their own place where they can retire if given the command to do so. They should be discouraged from running after vehicles and accepting food from strangers.

A major rule when training sheep dogs is not to restrict their readiness to attack, if there is the possibility they may need it during their work. Young dogs should not get into fights with stronger ones or they will lose their self-confidence.

Sheep dogs must be taught to ignore game and poultry. They should not be encouraged to catch mice and rats, and should be kept away from the tracks of game so they do not follow that scent instead of the herd or flock.

Sheep dogs have also guarding tasks, but these should not be taught until the animal is over 12 months old. This includes training the animal to "stay", "sit", detain people and guard a fenced-off area by either barking when somebody enters or attacking without any sound. Here the command "attention" or "watch out" is used. When strangers arrive, the dog should bark. A dog trained to attack must always be strictly controlled by the owner. The systematic training of sheep dogs should start after they are 6 months old. In general, they are not used for really serious work before they are 2 years old. It is a good system to have two dogs guarding the herd, as the older dog will help in the training of the younger. If the shepherd has two well-trained dogs, it is advisable to keep one of them on a leash so that it does not wander off.

When training the animal to round up and guard the herd, the object is for the dog to run round the perimeter and not criss-cross the herd, as later on it will be difficult to discourage bad habits, and instead of rounding up it may scatter the herd. The dog should be encouraged with the commands "catch", "drive on" to carry out its task. On highways, where there is heavy traffic, the herd should be driven on the right side. If there are two shepherd dogs, one should take to the middle of the road, paying attention that the left side be clear, while the other flanks the herd on the edge of the road. A dog can be guided by vocal commands, gestures, a whistle or a combination of all these.

A good shepherd dog can keep a herd together all by itself. It will walk round it from time to time and then sit beside its master, watching the herd's movement and awaiting its master's commands. After a dog has acquired an elementary discipline it is the shepherd's task to give his animal a special tuition necessary for given circumstances and his own requirements. For instance, the dog should know the forbidden and dangerous spots where the herd should not graze. It should know in which direction the herd has to be driven for watering, and while they drink it should take good care that they do not disperse.

Training Guard Dogs

When selecting a guard dog the first decision is the breed. Do we want a small or a big dog, for instance? If we only need a warning dog a smaller but "noisy" type should do. If, however, the dog is requested to watch and guard property, it will need to be a big dog.

Training should be started as soon as possible. Besides the already described basic schooling, one should aim at training to be courageous and to be distrustful of strangers.

Courage cannot be induced in a dog if it is naturally timid. To overcome "puppy fears" one should try to accustom the young animal to artificially created noises, while patting and quieting it gently, and it should be comforted and reassured every time it is frightened by something.

Suspicion is an important feature of good guard dogs. One of the major requirements of a guard dog is that he should mistrust people entering the house or garden until he sees his master is friendly. Do not permit your dog to go up to strangers, to play and be friendly with unknown people. At the same time do not let the animal get too wild, as for any accident caused by the dog its master is responsible. Guard dogs are supposed to signal the arrival of callers by barking, and it should discourage people from entering the house without permission. However, dogs should be taught not to bark excessively at any passer-by. If reprimanded by its master a few times, it will sooner or later learn when it is supposed to bark. Some watch dogs will, without special training, permit strangers to enter their territory, but will prevent from leaving it by standing close to the stranger and growling.

An important task is to induce watchfulness and attention. A number of methods are known and a time-tested and successful one is to ask a stranger to make a noise at some distance from the master; the dog is supposed to guard, while we encourage our dog to watchfulness by commanding "watch out". This exercise has to be repeated several times. It goes without saying that care should be taken lest the animal cause anybody damage while learning to guard.

II. HUNGARIAN SHEEP DOGS
A) HERDING SHEEP DOGS

The Puli

(Canis familiaris ovilis villosus hungaricus. Raitsits, 1924*)*

The Puli is the ancient sheep dog of Hungary. He has worked sheep on the plains of the Puszta since the 9th century, and has survived quite simply because he was, and still is, physically and temperamentally superlative for the work. Although the breed has undergone some changes through the centuries, all the prime qualities of the Puli have been transmitted to the dogs we have today.

The nomadic shepherds were always aware of the value of a good working companion: they kept two types of dog, the big white guard dogs who took over care of the flock at night, and the small active sheep dog, the Puli, who actually worked the flock by day. The shepherds protected the characteristics of their dogs by taking care that the two types did not cross-breed, and by ruthlessly culling out weak specimens. Through generations the shepherds carefully guarded the greatest values of their Pulis: ability and readiness to work. They did not pay too much attention to the dog's outward appearance, colour, marks, coat texture; to have a willing, keen intelligent dog was the most important to them. They could not tolerate a slack dog and so carried a natural long-term selection for breeding. It has been noted that shepherds were willing to give their whole year's salary for a good dog—which were sometimes well above today's prices. A shepherd who took pride in his job would boast of his clever Puli, who was more than just a dog in his eyes. But again a Puli was immediately downgraded into being a dog, and was easily got rid of, even killed, as soon as he proved unsatisfactory in everyday working tasks.

This consistent ruthless culling through the centuries helped to achieve the high standards of the breed today. It is not necessary to submit the Puli to a long, special training: after having observed once or twice a rounding-up, he is able to perform this activity with great accuracy himself. He is capable of learning other tasks with great ease. The last fifty years have seen the Puli adapt to life in towns and flats, while more interest has been taken in his colour, coat and shape. Fortunately, his intelligence and eagerness for work has not diminished, and when he returns to a rural environment, he easily switches back to being the complete sheep dog.

The name Puli, meaning a sheep dog, appears in Hungarian literature in 1751 for the first time.

The first descriptions of Hungarian sheep dogs date back to Ferenc Páriz-

Pápai (1708 and 1767), Ferenc Pethe (1815), and Friedrich Treitschke (1840), but in the 1800s the names Puli and Pumi were not clearly separated.

Controlled breeding began in the 1910s. This was the period when experts in natural sciences began to give a lead in breeding Hungarian sheep dogs. First of all Dr. Emil Raitsits* deserves the credit for giving a precise description of the breeds. Later on other experts followed his example and defined the ideal breeding programme (1920). The description of the Puli in those days was as follows: "A type of medium size sheep dog whose body is covered with a shaggy, matting coat. His drooping ears are also covered with long hair. Bright, intelligent eyes are hardly visible behind the falls of hair on the head. The hair on the tail—which curls back over the loins—is long. The limbs are also covered with long, wavy hair. The hair on the loins and on the hind legs becomes easily matted. He is lively, very alert, nimble, faithful, loyal and most apt to learn." The Puli, as far as his inner qualities are concerned, is very consistent. His outward appearance, on the other hand, has gone through many changes during the course of time. We are going to illustrate with photographs the traceable, ancient variations of the Puli. After having examined the photographs and the descriptions, it would be interesting to investigate what changes occurred in his characteristics, size, hair and colour, up to our days.

To guard the sheep it was necessary to have a fast moving, lean dog. The ancient Puli's head—as illustrations show—was longer than that of his modern counterpart, his nose more pointed and he had more or less pricked ears. Only after 1920—when the Pumi was identified as a separate breed—did the Puli's presently accepted shape of head become dominant, i.e., a rounder form with a shorter nose and drooping ears.

The variations in the Puli's size can be explained by its work. If bred for guarding sheep the ideal height is about 40 cm. Pulis of 40–50 cm proved to be more useful with cattle and pigs. Pulis over 50 cm were used by the police between the two world wars as guard dogs. Small and dwarf Pulis, 30 cm tall, can only be pets. The modern standard only accepts one height, because Pulis are now less frequently used for guarding sheep, and more often as watchdogs or household pets. This puts the ideal height between 34 and 43 cm.

Sometimes the Pulis that are considered the most attractive have hair that fills the space between trunk, limbs and the ground. Naturally, such long hair would have hampered the Pulis' work. We know that the Puli of 100 years ago did not have such a long coat. Shorter hair was necessary to ensure free movement and quick turning of the head. It is known that shepherds often sheared their Pulis at the same time as the sheep, but the shaggy, matted coat gave such good protection during winter that even the worst cold of the Puszta—the Hungarian

---

* Raitsits, Emil Dr., professor of the Veterinary College, leading Hungarian expert on animal breeding from the early 1900s, author of many articles on the same subject between 1916 and 1933.

Plains—could not harm the Puli. Thick, but not too long coat was essential even in the early days, but now the preference is a cord-like matted or fully corded coat covering the head and limbs.

There has always been a lot of argument about the colour of the Puli. Shepherds considered the character of their dogs to be the most important factor, and were hardly interested in coat colour. The larger guard dogs, the Komondor and the Kuvasz, who worked on the edge of the flock, were required to be white, so that the shepherd could easily distinguish them from a wolf, even at night. The Puli, on the other hand, was multi-coloured, in the strictest sense of the word. Fifty years ago it was even believed that black Pulis were not thoroughbred, as they were a rare minority colour.

Selective breeding first eliminated brown pigmentation of the skin, and particolouring. The number of colour variations became less and less. Finally, during the 1940s, the belief was widespread that only pure black Pulis without any marks were thoroughbred and only these could be used in breeding. Puppies of other colours were born as well, but breeders quickly culled these as they were considered a hindrance to the purity of the breed.

Today all breeders aim to achieve whole colour with grey pigmented skin. They try to breed the different colours separately, always avoiding inter-breeding. It would be a pity to lessen the diversity of the Puli by eliminating the different colours. Although black is now the best known colour, white Pulis have become rather numerous in the last ten years. Other accepted colours are grey and cream (apricot), but these have not yet been officially separated from black.

Standardization and Valuation of the Puli

The aim of standardization is to help in forming a uniform breed. At the same time it helps to eliminate cross-breeding and the deterioration of the type. Before there were breed standards, breeds often got mixed-up (Pumi, Puli, Mudi). It happened even at dog-shows that prick-eared, short-haired, pointed-headed dogs were presented as Pulis. Breeders themselves were not quite sure of the basic requirements that could rightly be expected of each and every Puli.

Experts in animal breeding knew that the only possibility of rationalizing the individual qualities of all the herding sheep dogs was by describing the characteristics of each breed. The first separate description of Pulis and Pumis comes from 1902. Dr. Raitsits gave a detailed study of standards in 1924. This study was later accepted by the FCI as well. The basic requirements of this standard are still valid, but because life constantly changes, new aims also appeared in breeding sheep dogs, and new standard descriptions had to be laid down. The new standard was accepted by the FCI and has been entered as the 1966/No.55/b standard. The study establishes the results that were achieved in breeding, and, to a certain extent, outlines the possibilities for the future.

Breed characteristics include both the outward appearance (colour, hair, shape) and the intellectual qualities (readiness to work, herding ability, hardiness, ability to learn). One must strictly differentiate between the two groups of characteristics. Ever since the breeding of Pulis was taken over by enthusiastic breeders, regulations for judging appearance have become more exacting. During the last 30 years Pulis have become more uniform in appearance. Standards of inner qualities have changed less. Today the Puli is still expected to be keen to work, to adapt well to his environment and the climate, to be a hardy dog who can do well on simple food; a dog which will show great intelligence, not only in herding sheep but also in guarding property.

The good natural qualities of the Pulis have resulted in acknowledgement and approval of the breed from all over the world.

Judging the Appearance

Non-experts will always judge a dog by its appearance. Even hobby-breeders often concentrate only on the exterior, because this enables them to achieve quicker results. It is strange to see that, although for long centuries the temperament of these sheep dogs was the most important factor, the breed became well-known all over the world only after selective breeders had evolved the distinctive type of the modern Puli.

Looks and performance should, however, not be divided! Let us attempt to create a breed that is attractive to look at and fit for its purpose. Selective breeding demands this, and it cannot put the importance of temperament and ability in second place. Appearance will have to go hand in hand with qualities that enable this breed to carry out its specialised work. Breeders ought to know not only the anatomical structure of the dog but will also have to be acquainted with the physical functions, before deciding that changing them through breeding will improve the dog.

General Appearance

The Puli is a dog of medium size, vigorous, alert and tough, with a sound square body. His long coat gives him a special place in dog society. He does not impress by a beautifully clean-cut shape, but by his distinctive shaggy appearance.

He is built of sinewy joints and fine bones. Over-refined dogs are just as undesirable as those with a coarse structure. Head, neck and ears are covered with long hair which blends in with the body, not showing noticeably separate features. The tail curls back over the hindquarters. The real shape of the hindquarters cannot be seen because of the long hair covering the tail. Falls of hair also fill the space between the front and hind legs, sometimes reaching to the ground.

After the first year of a Puli's life it is impossible to distinguish the individual parts of his body; to judge conformation will only be possible by handling. He stands fore-square, his movements are quick and bouncy, his gait short stepping and brisk. He should not be too noisy, despite his very lively temperament. He must be tough and very sound.

Description of the Parts of the Body

Head. From the front it appears to be round, from the side slightly egg-shaped. The thick hair on the head of an adult Puli overshadows the eyes like an awning. The skull is slightly domed, the muzzle gives 30 per cent of the length of the whole head. The stop is clearly defined, the nasal bone straight. The arches above the eye are prominent. The nose is slightly blunt, the nostrils relatively large, but never coarse or fleshy. The upper and lower jaw-bones are both fully developed. If they are not developed equally or not fitted properly, faults show up with the bite, and this is strongly hereditary. The bigger the gap between the upper and lower incisors, the more serious the fault, as the strength of the hold is in jeopardy.

The Puli's teeth are regular and strong. The scissors bite is ideal if the front teeth (incisors) of the upper jaw just cover the front teeth of the lower jaw. A level bite is not as perfect as the scissors, but acceptable. Overshot or undershot mouths are considered serious faults, and such dogs should not be used for breeding. Underdeveloped or crooked teeth, or uneven rows of incisors are also undesirable. In the old days it was customary to cut off the sharp points of the canine teeth so that the Puli could not harm the sheep, but this custom has died out completely as the bite of a trained Puli is gentle. This mutilation of the teeth must be regarded as cruelty. The lips are not fleshy and fit tight to the teeth.

A coarse head betrays a coarse physique and a phlegmatic, stolid temperament. This is much against the typical character and thus should be avoided, but, on the other hand, a pointed head and small nostrils indicate inter-breeding with the Spitz family. A too deep stop shows the influence of poodles or Maltese dogs. If the temporal bones are not well enough developed the head is narrow and pointed. The longer the nose the more serious the fault. Loose lips are a sign of slackness of physique.

Ears are set medium high and are pendent. They are not seen among the hair, and are not pricked up even when the dog is alert. The flap is broad and has the shape of a rounded-off V, extending to the inner corner of the eye.

Ears that differ from the ideal in shape, size, or setting are to be treated as serious faults, because the shape of the ears is hereditary and clearly shows generation after generation. This is the reason why dogs with prick ears, droopy, outsize, fleshy or small, pointed ears have to be excluded from breeding.

Eyes should be coffee-brown or black and free of discharge. Sometimes loose hair gets under the eyelids and causes inflammation, in this case a veterinary surgeon should be consulted. Lids have to be tight. Slack eyelids are certain to be inherited; a serious fault. Protruding, elongated eyes are not desirable. The look is lively, honest, intelligent.

Light brown eyes, yellow or blue iris, wall eyes (white iris), eyes of different colour—all are alien to the breed, and are serious faults.

The *neck* is muscular, of medium length, set in an angle of 45° to the horizontal. When held horizontally, the head, the neck and the back show a straight line. A poodle-like, steep angulation of the neck is undesirable.

The real length of the neck can hardly be felt. If the neck is too obvious it is a sign of some fault. A long neck is normally less muscular. The sharp upper line of a scrawny neck continues generally in weak withers and back. The *withers* rise only slightly over the back line. Weak withers are a fault, which usually goes with a flat chest. Hair tends to separate on an edgy neckline and narrow withers. If the shoulders are loose the back tends to slack behind the withers. In more serious cases this slacking can be detected even in front of the withers. This shows softness of the physique. If the dog is still young this fault can be corrected by lots and lots of exercise.

The *back* must be straight and of medium length. If it exceeds the ideal length it makes the Puli look too long and lose his square shape. Long backs, dipping or saddle backs are serious faults and a sign of weakness.

A most important requirement is the straightness, shortness and tightness of the *loins*. Long and sunken loins a most serious fault, cannot be overlooked.

One of the present day requirements is the tail carried over the back, curled and pressed against the loins. It makes judging a Puli's *hindquarters* in show-position rather difficult, but if a dog carries his tail low, it changes the shape of the hindquarters altogether. A broad *croup* is an especially important requirement with bitches.

The upper thighbone should meet the pelvis at an angle of 90°. Any variation of this angle is undesirable. A flat, sloped croup mostly meets inadequately angulated hind legs; on the other hand a too flat croup and stiff legs may result in a high-set vulva—and the bitch will be a problem to mate.

Pulis with ideal *tail carriage* seem to be higher at the rump but most of the time this proves to be a mere optical illusion. A "sickle-tail" is tolerated but a straight tail or a permanently hanging one is a serious fault.

When judging the tail carriage of a Puli, let us remember that dogs carry their tails low or even hold them between their legs in a strange environment or when frightened. But as soon as they are back to familiar surroundings and are relaxed the inherited tail carriage is taken up immediately. Therefore, tail carriage should be judged carefully at shows as it is not the momentary appearance that is important, but the inherited setting of the tail.

Some Pulis are born with short tails or tailless. This is a serious, hereditary fault. It is important to withdraw not only these Pulis but also their parents from breeding.

The *chest*. A broad, long and deep chest is desirable. Flat-chested Pulis, narrow in front, are not suitable for breeding.

The *belly* is slightly drawn up. Two lines of 4–5 nipples will provide the milk when the pups arrive. Hair should be clipped around the mammary glands before whelping, so that the puppies can get at them easily. Some bitches who have had several litters may have nipples that are bigger than normal even after they have stopped feeding the puppies. It is important to make sure that the puppies can take the whole of the nipple in their mouths, otherwise they may not get enough milk. Flat-chested bitches do not make good mothers.

Genitals must be entire.

Monorchids are nearly unknown in Pulis, but nevertheless it is better to check the presence of both testicles when buying a dog.

Limbs. Loosely attached shoulder blades, which can occur through lack of tight muscle ligaments, are unacceptable. In a young puppy loose shoulders can be improved by regular exercise.

The Puli's shoulders are rather steep. The upper arm should meet the shoulder blade at an angle of 90°, and should not be out at elbow or withdrawn under the trunk. The elbows should be parallel with the body. If the elbows point outward and the paws are turned in—the dog is "out at elbow". If the elbows turn in and the paws are pointing outward, we talk of a "fiddle-front". The first fault obstructs the Puli in his swift movement, while the latter is an indication of too narrow a chest.

The forelegs must be straight and true.

Joints should not be rough or enlarged. Swollen joints are the result of a faulty metabolism, especially in young puppies.

The *pastern* is responsible for the springy action of the Puli. Steep pasterns do not absorb the jolts and jerks, but with soft pasterns, all the weight is carried by the sinews and ligaments. Ideally, the angle of the pastern should be approximately 45°, but this is nearly impossible to detect on Pulis except by handling. Serious faults on the legs are noticeable, and they have to be severely judged.

The *feet* are short, rounded and tight. The claws are hard, not overlong, on well developed pads. Feet should be parallel; toeing in or out is equally undesirable.

The hocks should be straight and strong. Several *malformations of the legs* can occur with Pulis. On the *forelegs:* elbows in or out, narrow front, bowed legs, feet pointing in or outward, splay foot which is frequently the result of a fault in structure, soft pasterns, weak toes.

On the *hindquarters:* steep hindquarters when the stifles do not form a right angle; bowlegs and toeing in, cowhocks; toeing out—sometimes to the extent that the hocks nearly touch.

The skin. The Puli's skin contains much pigment, it is black, blueish-black or slate-grey. The colour of the skin can also be detected amongst the hair, but it is easier to see on the hairless parts of the body—eyelids, nostrils, lips, pads. These all have to be black. Due to long selective breeding we cannot tolerate either spots of lighter colour, or lighter colouring of these parts. The palate is uniformly darkgrey or a variety of deep-pigmented spots on a dark base colour, the tongue always bright red. The iris must have dark pigmentation, black or brown. Claws have to be black or grey. The belly should be uniformly pigmented.

Marks, showing lack of pigmentation, and a yellow or light-blue iris must exclude a Puli from breeding, as such faults of pigmentation may reappear in future generations and be difficult to eliminate. A small white patch of white hair on the chest not more than 5 cm in diameter can be tolerated but a larger mark is a serious fault.

Skin colour of grey, white, cream Pulis must carry the same dark pigmentation.

Coat. The Puli's coat is striking and highly characteristic. It appears in a great variety of shapes and forms, it can be given new styles and re-shaped. The artistic sense and creativity of human beings can find real fulfilment here. It is likely that the Puli's popularity and the enormous interest in breeding them is largely due to its exciting and original coat. The Puli's coat can have many forms depending purely on the percentage of the different kinds of hair present. In general the proportion of hair decides the kind of grooming the coat needs.

When looking carefully in the coat, parting the hair we see many little curls that break from under the skin in small tufts. These curls consist of rough *upper-hair* and finer wool.

The soft undercoat does not contain medullary substance. It is very fine and largely blends in with the upper-hair. The upper-hair which does contain medullary substance is rougher, more wiry and much longer. The upper hair and the undercoat are not always noticeably different.

Puli hair has a very special feature; the diameter of each hair can vary within the hair's length, wider in places and narrower at others. The medullary substance breaks off in the very thin sections of the hair, which bend, shrink and break easily. "Thinning" is the reason for extensive shagginess. Dead hair does not fall out of the coat because of shrinkage but gets matted and causes the felting of the coat.

The length of hair varies on the different parts of the body. The hair is longest on the tail and on the croup (8–18 cm), shorter on the back, the hindlegs, the chest and the flanks (6–10 cm), even shorter on the neck, forelegs (6–8 cm) and shortest on the head and paws (4–6 cm).

The hair of a new-born puppy is short, approximately 0.5–1 cm; glossy, either curly, or wavy, sometimes even straight. A few days old puppy can be curly to such an extent that he looks astrakhan.

Puppies change their hair twice. At first while they are still on the dam, when a thick, slightly wavy, very fine, 4–6 cm long, teddy-bear like coat replaces the shorter, shiny coat. This fluffy puppy-hair slowly hides the different parts of the body making it more difficult to see the puppy's build and to judge its proportions. The quality and shape of the puppy's hair is not permanent. False judgements can be made and sometimes it is safer to form an opinion while the puppy is still on the dam than a short while after.

As the puppy grows older he changes his hair once more (9–11 months). Dogs mature enough for breeding, i.e. 14–16 months old, show their adult hair—but naturally the coat is not fully developed. It will be in six months time, during which the length of the coat and its shape can be expected to show great changes. A Puli's coat looks its best when the Puli is 2 years old, and it stays roughly the same until he is 6 or 7.

As mentioned, there are many types of coats, depending partly on the structure of the hair but also on the kind of grooming. We refer to shaggy, matted in plates, matted in wide-ribbons, matted in small ribbons, corded, wavy curly, open (straight), silky, and short hair. It can be ungroomed, groomed, well-groomed, and over-groomed, and these can all occur within each different type of hair.

Before discussing each type of hair in detail, we should like to mention the two different opinions about the original type of the Puli's coat. Some experts believe that the original shape is the matted coat, which gave them protection once and gives the real characteristic of the breed today, any other formation being undesirable. Nevertheless, heavy, armour-like matted coats were considered faulty. Other experts favoured the corded coat, which is more attractive and has become more fashionable nowadays. The proportion of the top coat and the fine wool determines the formation of the coat. Pulis with a corded coat are undoubtedly pure bred; corded hair has to be considered simply as one formation of the coat. The two extreme kinds, corded and matted, have not yet been bred separately.

Because of the Puli's growing popularity, it is essential to establish all we know about his coat texture.

Shagginess is due to the predominance of fine fluff which causes severe matting. If this is completely neglected, felt-like mats, knots, tangles are formed with no obvious construction. The matted hair sometimes forms a heavy, plating coat, mainly on the hindquarters, but also on the body and the neck. It can only be got rid of by cutting off the hair completely.

Pulis with a *matted coat* have lots of fine fluffy hair and less of the rougher coat. The hair tangles and felts in the same way as we described before, but the mats are smaller, much flatter and are distributed more evenly over the body. We shall explain later how coats of this kind can be untangled and looked after. A disadvantage of this hair structure is that the matted plates can develop again very soon, so plenty of time must be spent on regular grooming to keep the coat tidy. Then there are the Pulis, whose hair mats by itself into irregular, *wide ribbons*. These sausage-shaped felt cords can move freely and keep their shape without special grooming. The quantity of fine fluff is too high so it mats several curls together.

When the felt cords are rather flat and not wider than a man's finger, and evenly cover the whole body, we speak of a *small-ribbon* coat. This feature can be maintained without much care. If unkempt, some curls can still mat together.

A *corded coat* will develop when a Puli grows mainly top coat. The pencil-thick cords will take shape quite by themselves, without any grooming and will stay unchanged for a lifetime, never felting, just growing longer.

A Puli may appear in a *short, curly coat* but only temporarily, i.e., after moulting or having been shorn. The Puli must have a long coat, so individuals with a permanently short coat should be omitted from breeding.

An *open coat* is wrong! Some people—mainly in foreign countries—think that a really well-kept dog has to be combed right through. This may be the case with Afghans and Poodles but it is a big mistake to comb and brush a Puli's coat till fluffy, like a Poodle's. Unfortunately there are also open coats that are not the result of over-grooming but of genetically unsuitable hair, for instance, too silky or too rough and straight hair. If the hair is not curly but is only slightly wavy, it will never be able to felt into ribbons or cords.

Incorrect hair structure will be passed on to the succeeding generations, so dogs with this type of coat are strictly banned from breeding.

Grooming of the hair. Even when used for herding the flocks, Pulis were not allowed to have too shaggy, heavily felted coats. The shepherds sheared off the excess coat as it was a nuisance for the dogs to carry. Today, regular grooming is used instead of scissors to keep the Puli's hair in shape. The appearance of the Puli improved greatly by being kept as companions in villages, towns and flats. If a "puszta" Puli is brought nowadays to an international show, he stands out from amongst well-groomed Pulis as if they were not of the same breed.

It soon became obvious that certain coat formations needed hardly any grooming at all while others had to be attended to daily. Naturally, selective breeding favoured the coat that showed the best shape with the least amount of work.

The attractive shape of a corded coat can be maintained with very little work. It is enough to give it a light brush once a week to remove any dirt from between the cords.

It is possible to turn even a wide-ribboned coat into a corded coat. One just has to watch that not too many curls stick together, and get felted. There are experts who consider the ribbon-like hair formation acceptable—even ideal—and treat it in the same way as the corded coat, and clean it just once a week. To prevent matting—if the adult hair shows signs of this process, or if the newly-grown hair starts to become felted—one has to tear the felted mats apart into ribbons or cords right up to the skin.

1 Black Puli dog, with small, well-proportioned head and corded type coat

2 Four-week-old black Puli puppies
3 Five-week-old white Puli puppy

4 Two-month-old black Puli puppies
5 Seven-week-old black and white Puli puppies from the same litter

6 Ten-week-old black Puli puppies from the same litter
7 One-year-old grey Puli dog
8 Seven-month-old grey Puli bitch
9 Seven-month-old cream Puli bitch

10 Black Puli dog, corded coat, with a too long body trunk

11 Well coupled six-year-old black Puli bitch with a ribbon-type coat. The bitch has had several litters

15 The felted mats are taken apart
16 The end of the tangles has to be found...
17 .....and pulled apart.....
18 .....up to the skin
19 Untangling a felted coat starts by slicing up the mats, beginning from the skin

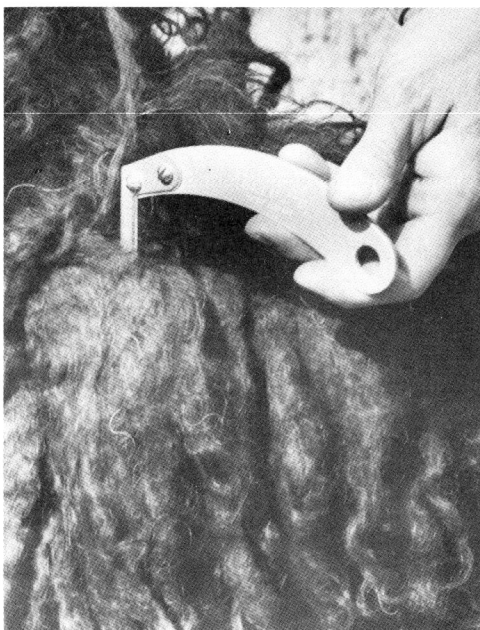

14 Well-groomed, two-year-old black Puli dog with ribbon-type coat

15–19 Grooming the coat of Pulis with matted hair

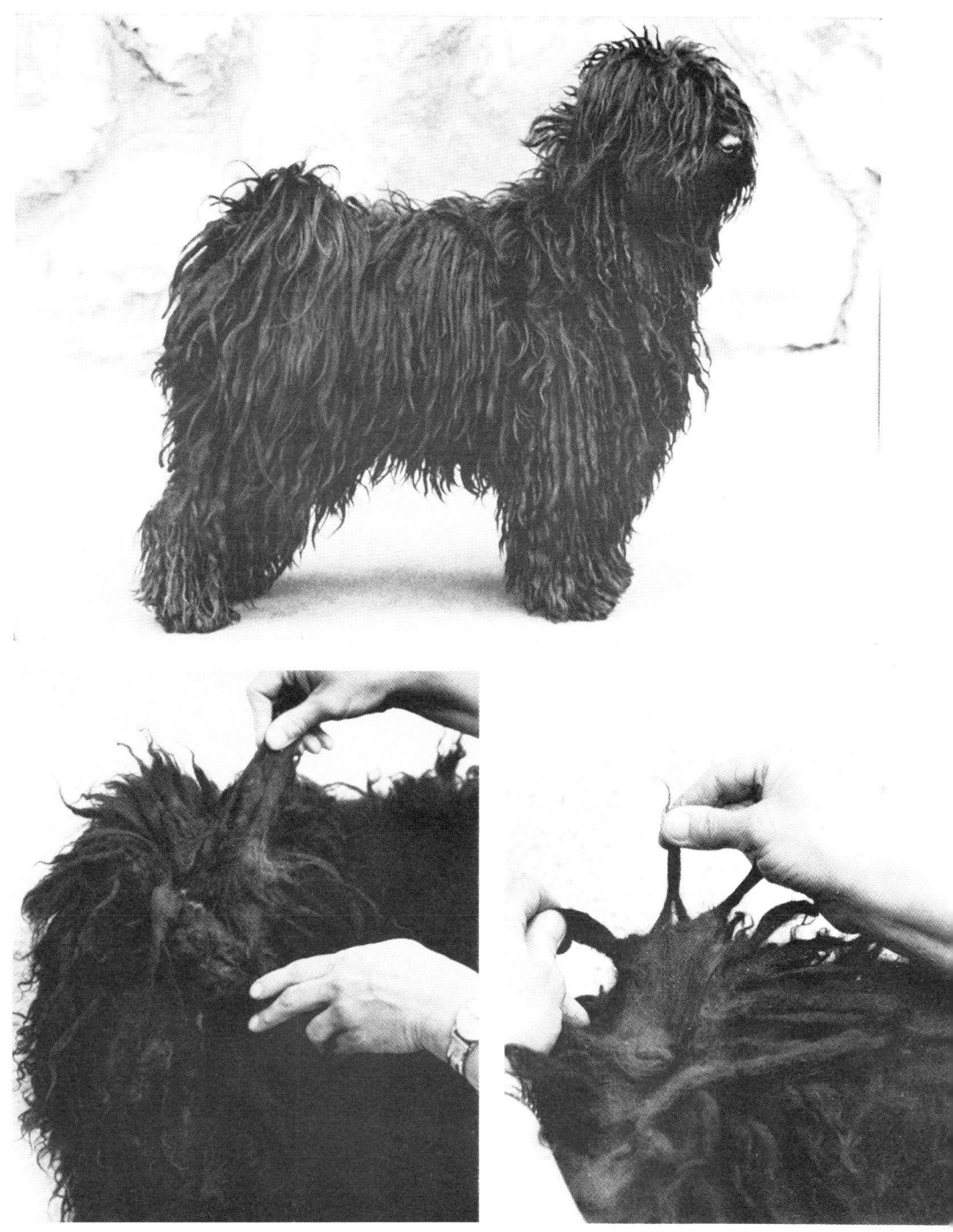

12 Ideal structure two-and-a-half-year old black Puli dog with well-groomed, corded coat

13 Ideal structure, one-year-old Puli dog with corded coat

20 Corded Puli coat, top left
21 Corded Puli coat, top right
22 Wide-ribbon Puli coat, middle left
23 Ribbon-type Puli coat, middle right
24 Tangled, ungroomed Puli coat, bottom left
25 Curly puppy-Puli coat, bottom right
26 Ungroomed, matted Puli coat
27 Well-groomed Puli bitch with a corded-type coat. International champion

28 Three-year-old grey Puli bitch with wide-ribbon coat
29 Puli guarding the herd
30 A well-proportioned ribbon-coated Puli dog with a round, small head and profuse locks shading the eyes

31 After careful grooming a broad-ribbon-type coat may get a corded character

32 A well-coupled two-year-old black Puli dog with a narrow ribbon coat

31 After careful grooming a broad-ribbon-type coat may get a corded character

32 A well-coupled two-year-old black Puli dog with a narrow ribbon coat

33 An excellent Puli bitch of 18 months with a white, corded coat

34 This is still a puppy-coat; later on eyes and muzzle are covered by locks and fringes
35 An ideal, wide-postured black Puli

Always halve the cords, and continue to do this until each is the thickness of a pencil. Torn up, the ribbons look loose, but will take up a definite shape within a few days. These cords will not have quite the rounded form as may be seen on dogs whose coat is naturally corded, but will show more of a flat, ribbon-like appearance, which may be considered an even more attractive formation.

It is not enough to do this work once but care must be taken to prevent the matting occurring again. It varies with each individual dog whether tearing up is necessary once a year, once a month, or even more frequently.

Never use a wire brush. Brushing should not break up the shape of cords. There is a group of breeders in the USA who comb and brush the hair until the coat becomes completely fluffy, but this style does not suit the original character of the Puli.

Grooming a matted coat is a most difficult task, as it is not usually possible to break up the outer mats and work towards the inside of the coat. If tearing up the cords by hand proves impossible, they may be cut up. It is better to start with the loose hair next to the skin, and then slice the mats into ribbons either with a razor or scissors. Pulis who have just been through a treatment of this sort do not look very attractive at first but after a few days, when the hair has settled, it can be worked through by hand to give it a natural appearance.

Where such drastic grooming is required special attention must be paid to the tail. Sometimes hair on the tail gets matted more quickly than on the rest of the body, so the tail has to be groomed, too.

A very heavily matted coat can most easily be dealt with by simply cutting off the mats, that is, by shearing the whole dog. The new hair will have to be arranged into curls shortly after the plates have been removed, to avoid new felting.

Whelping and lactating bitches sometimes shed their coat partially or entirely. This is because the body gets less nourishment than under normal circumstances, so it gets rid of the hair on the neck, shoulders, sometimes the front of the body or, less frequently, all over the body. After the hormone balance has readjusted, the bitch grows a new coat of healthy hair. As shedding is often due to hormone imbalance, this may explain hairless male dogs, too.

Coat shedding is only temporary. It is inconvenient only if the Puli is to be presented at a show but cannot win because of lack of the coat.

Pulis of certain families lose their coat easily, but there are others whose members can have many litters without shedding their coat at all. Understandably, these families are very valuable to the breeder.

Colour of hair. We have already mentioned that the Puli originally was a breed of many colours. The story of the Puli's colour can be closely followed from earliest entries in the pedigree registration books.

When scientists and experts in breeding began to take an interest in Pulis at the beginning of the 1920s, the following colours were found: white, cream-coloured, dove-grey, silver grey, olive grey, pale yellow, blue grey, slate, iron grey, steel blue, faded black, rusty black, black with intermixture of white, and sometimes even jet black. To breed exclusively black, was a trend which began only thirty years ago.

Black, being a dominant colour, spread very easily. Black Pulis were favoured in breeding, if their black colour was homozygous even when mated to heterozygous Pulis, always giving black puppies in the first generation.

This explains the great speed with which black colour spread. Although later generations threw back to other colours, these were not used for breeding, because the breeders acted under the influence of the current fashion, and were ashamed to have puppies of other colours than black.

Due to this misguided policy, colour variations were rarely found by 1950. The standard description of 1960 describes the ideal colour as black.

This flow of black colour—which is an example of breeding based on wrong principles—was interrupted by the appearance of white Pulis in the early 1960s. Grey was more readily accepted by official opinion, as the black hair of most Pulis fades into grey as years go by.

A revision of the standard description in 1966 says: "Pulis are of different colours. Black, several shades of grey and white are bred at present." From then on puppies of whole colours were left alive, no matter what the colour was.

White very soon became popular as it is a most attractive colour. The FCI has just recently acknowledged white Pulis as a separate colour which should not be interbred with any other colour.

We consider the return to breeding other colours as well as black a very fortunate tendency, which will enrich the breed and help its popularity. Let us breed different colours by employing careful selective breeding. It is most important therefore, to be familiar with the genetic principles of colour.

Brown colouring is alien to the breed but sometimes it still reappears, accompanied by brown pigmentation of the skin. Young dogs with chocolate brown hair do not meet the standard of the breed.

There are two different types of white coat. First, there are puppies born with a true white coat, these are the genetically white dogs. In the second type the puppy is born with creamy off-white hair, and only grows a pure white coat later in life. Pulis belonging to the second group always maintain certain marks that betray their original colour. For example: the ears are yellow, newly grown hair looks yellowish, and the roots of the hair show signs of yellow. To begin with we shall discuss the heredity of the genetically white colour.

White hair is recessive in comparison to black. Black parents can only produce white puppies if they both carry the genes of white colour.

Today white Pulis are not interbred with dogs of any other colour.

Ever since international breeding of white Pulis was introduced it has happened that instead of or alongside with white puppies, cream Pulis were born. These cream puppies came in all shades, from off-white to apricot colours. The appearance of the cream colour is not really a new development because the colour range of the Puli originally included cream variations. When puppies of darker colours were born in a white litter, breeders did not register them but the off-whites and light cream-coloured ones were allowed to be used for breeding, as the breeders hoped to produce white puppies from them. Off-white seemed to be closest to white and Pulis with a very light cream coat were known to have faded into white as they grew older. But experience showed that there are four or five different shades of cream and breeding of these shades is carefully planned nowadays. Cream compared to black has recessive genes and appears to be homozygotic. Once we observed an interesting case where two cream Pulis were mated and there were black puppies in the litter. A more careful examination of both animals showed that the sire was not a true homozygotic cream specimen. (The coloured photograph shows this dog.) The black mask, dark ears and the black intermingled hair make it clear that he carries the gene for black pigment as well, so he has to be considered a black heterozygote. Knowing this, we arranged to mate him with two other cream bitches and, as expected (due to the principles of genetics)—only 50% of the new-born puppies were cream while the other 50% were black.

Research has shown that it is impossible to breed white Pulis from cream parents. On the other hand, off-white (really cream ones) can produce puppies of a deeper cream colour.

The depth of shade is determined by a doubling up of the gene-chain, which can produce offspring in a wide range of tones. Off-white dogs which acquire their colour because of this fact do not pass on their colour to the next generation as a rule, so they do not breed true.

Grey-coated Pulis are either born with hair of a dirty, greyish colour, or the coat fades into grey as the dog grows older. Detailed studies of their genetics cannot yet be carried out because of the small number of grey-coated Pulis left after World War II.

Using the results of research the colour genetics of the Puli can be arranged according to their effectiveness: black, grey, white, cream. The cream as separate colour—being at the end of the epistatic line—can be easily maintained in further breeding.

The modern tendency is to eliminate all kinds of marks and patches of colours. A white patch on the chest not exceeding 5 cm in diameter, and few white hairs between the toes can be allowed according to the standard description, but Pulis of solid colour are more desirable for breeding. None of the popular dogs used for breeding today have any marks or patches on their coats. Marks are inherited through dominant factors.

Greying cannot be mistaken for a white mark or patch. Greying is a common process with some Pulis and is a sign of aging. While the hairs of the white marks are rooted in pink skin which does not contain sufficient pigment, the white hairs of a greying Puli are still in heavily pigmented skin, alongside with the black hairs.

Scar-tissue sometimes produces white hair and the tissue itself that has been damaged by serious injury gets lighter in colour. White spots of this kind or the flesh-colour of scars are not hereditary, consequently cannot be judged as severely as an inherited patched coat. Dogs with marks from injuries might not get excellent critiques at shows but will not be handicapped in breeding.

Movement. We are interested in the movement of a Puli mainly because his movement indicates his temperament, as well as showing the action of the limbs and the way the whole body is carried. He has a short mincing step, quick, bouncy gallop, his action is gay and alert. We call the action perfect if the legs move straight forward, swinging, parallel to the sides without weaving or crabbing.

To judge the gait and the movements, the Puli is led towards the judge and then away in a straight line several times. Soft, loose joints of the limbs can be easily spotted this way. Then the judge has to examine the movement from the side view. A swaying top line means a soft back. The whole dog must seem to be tough and resilient, a roaching back or a saddle back are unacceptable.

Characteristics for Evaluation

On the previous pages we have been describing the different sections of the Puli's body. To complete the picture we have to consider further factors such as breed characteristics, sexual characteristics, proportions, development, condition and the inner qualities of temperament, ability to learn, etc. Neither the judge nor the breeder can be satisfied by taking into account only the outward appearance of a dog. To get the *full measure of the animal* the soundness of the structure, the type and condition will also have to be taken into consideration.

Breed Characteristics. A Puli must bear all the characteristics of his breed. If all the aforementioned outward characteristics can be found on a Puli he is a good type. Only dogs and bitches having typical characteristics can be used for breeding. It does happen sometimes that good quality puppies are born of poor bitches and dogs, but one should not rely on it and leave breeding to chance. Breeders should only use the best bitches and dogs.

By *sexual characteristics* we refer to the secondary sexual characteristics. Different housing systems, feeding routines and the different "blood-lines" can result in a great variety of looks, but it can be accepted as a rule that dogs are bigger with heavier bones and muscle than bitches.

The secondary sexual characteristics are determined by the animal's hormone activity. When secondary sexual characteristics are not distinct (an effeminate dog or coarsely built bitch), one must always relate this to the condition of the primary sexual characteristics. The poor quality of the secondary sexual characteristics is most certainly passed on to the new generation.

Conformation. A Puli has perfect proportions if all the different parts of his body are in harmony. None of the parts dominate the whole of the body but give a well-balanced shape.

A Puli is unbalanced if, for example, a fine body carries a large head. A dog with a very small, fine head is also out of proportion. Pulis with finely built bodies should not have rough hair. The front half of the body and the hindquarters should bear similar characteristics. The length of the body should correspond to the height of the withers. Pulis with long backs are disproportionate.

Bad proportions are difficult to correct even with a good choice of mate, as body shape is hereditary and, therefore, has to be judged very severely.

Development, muscular development. To judge each Puli fairly one must be fully acquainted with the average bodily measurements.

The uniformity of the breed demands one standard size. The great drop in the number of Pulis after World War II also proved this point.

Height of withers:	*males*
ideal height	40–44 cm
acceptable height	37–47 cm
	bitches
ideal height	37–41 cm
acceptable height	34–44 cm

If a dog is shorter than 34 cm or taller than 50 cm, or if a bitch is shorter than 31 cm or taller than 47 cm, they may not be used for breeding purposes.

Comparative size of the different parts of the body given as a percentage of the height of the withers:

	according to the standard description (minimum)	often
length of the trunk	100%	–
depth of the chest	45%	42–46
circumference of the chest	125%	117–120
width of the chest	33%	29–30
length of the head	45%	42–46
width of the croup	21%	20–22
circumference of the legs	20%	21
muzzle in proportion to the length of the head	35%	–
length of the ears in proportion to the length of the head	50%	–

Weight: males 13–15 kg; bitches 10–13 kg.

To be able to check the development of the puppies it is worth knowing how much weight they should gain.

The dogs of a litter usually weigh more than the bitches.

Weight of the puppies while still on the dam—in grams:

At birth	1	2	3	4	5	6	7
	weeks old							
140–300	350–500	550–800	850–1150	1250–1500	1650–2100	2100–2800	2600–3800

After weaning, the weight in kg.

At the age of	3	4	5	6	7	8	9
	months						
	4.1–6.0	4.9–7.8	5.6–9.4	6.3–10.9	6.9–10.9	7.3–11.2	7.8–11.5

When judging how well-developed each dog is one should not concentrate only on size but on all the physical features; from the condition of the teeth to the measurements of all parts of the body. A stocky, heavy body is not typical of Pulis. The ideal puppy has a fine-boned skeleton and lean and tough muscles. The dog should be seen moving as well as handled. One should not be misled by a temporary condition. Fat dogs are not muscular, but soft.

Condition. Refers to how well-fed and nourished the dog is. A Puli which is in perfect condition for breeding has no excess fat, but is lean and well muscled. Pulis presented at shows should be in slightly harder condition. A working Puli can be even leaner but loss of weight should not deteriorate into bad condition.

Temperament was determined by the work Pulis had to do through the centuries. A Puli had no chance of survival if he proved to be lazy, slack, or stolid in either herding the flock, or carrying out his duties in the farmyard. A lazy Puli was ruthlessly put down by the shepherd; and the same fate awaited the one that did not obey perfectly. Being lazy and unwilling to work was unforgiveable. This natural selection resulted in a healthy, vigorous temperament, and exceptions are very rare.

Lazy, slack Pulis should not be used for breeding.

To judge the temperament is difficult. At a show the judge is put in an unpleasant situation as he has to form an instant opinion. If a dog is alert and watches everything that happens around him, this is a good sign. Raitsits mentions an excellent test that was used by the shepherds to find out a Puli's temperament and to compare the qualities of different dogs. A Puli should bark if one squats down in front of him with a pebble or a piece of wood in one's hand, pretending to throw it away. If the dog does not show any excitement at all, does not bark and seems to be uninterested, its temperament falls below the standard.

Another good way to test a Puli's temperament is to watch how it reacts to a hidden source of sound.

Ability to learn. Shepherds say that a Puli does not have to be taught, for the ability to herd is in its blood. The truth is that the young puppy following its mother, sees and hears all it is required to do. It learns to obey orders without noticing it. It learns the connection between the words, intonation and the actual work without the slightest effort.

Natural selection worked wonders. Every Puli has an immense capacity for learning. When used for guarding homes it is acutely observant and is able to perform many minor tasks. It places people into two categories: pleasant ones and unpleasant ones.

It signals everyone's arrival to its master but does not keep a "friend" at bay for too long.

Pulis kept as pets have been known to understand and respond to 70 words but this can only be achieved by regular, patient teaching and training.

Once an American farmer went to town to fetch the vet to his cows which had bloat, taking his Puli with him. Next time, when the cows were once again bloated and its master was not at home, the Puli ran into town and kept barking at the vet's house until he understood what was the matter and quickly drove to the farm to save the cattle.

As Pulis are used less and less for herding, it is necessary to find other means to test their intelligence. Special training, sheep dog trials and other similar tests help us in assessing this side of a Puli's character.

Soundness. The inexhaustible ability to work can only be guaranteed by perfect condition. To judge this can prove a difficult task. Good muscle tone helps other characteristics to improve and makes reproduction easier.

Working Pulis were active from morning till night fulfilling their tasks. Dogs with slack bodies and poor health could not endure such conditions, and did not survive. Those that could cope with this harsh environment year after year flourished and multiplied.

Pulis, even though their bodies are of sound build, are still required to have fine bone. Coarsely built dogs are not popular.

Constitution is the amalgam of all the previously mentioned characteristics —the appearance, the function of the organs of the body and the dog's reactions to the stimuli from the outside world. This breed can be best described as having a sound but "fine" structure. Neither extreme—too fine nor coarse—is typical.

The Breeding of Pulis. Could there be a more exciting event for a family of Puli lovers than the time their bitch is whelping? How many puppies can be expected? What will they look like? One can hardly wait to see the puppies. Long anticipation leads up to the moment when finally, with relief, we can stroke the small, round head and say, "Well, Liz, you've been a very brave and clever girl". The honour, though, is not only hers, but is partly our own, because we are *breeders;* trying to unravel nature's secrets to improve our favourite breed.

To achieve even better results and have even more sound Pulis, we must understand how to make the right choice for breeding.

A Puli could prove his *ability* by working with the flock. The best way to test this is at a sheep dog trial. In the old days shepherds used to have these trials for sport. Written documents tell us that flocks of sheep were herded in and out of water, just to enable the shepherds to compare the ability of different Pulis. The Puli that worked well was always well respected, and people would come from far away to bring their dogs to mate with one of these famous Pulis, or have one of the new-born puppies. This natural selection helped to arrive at the uniformly high standard of the Puli's inner virtues—ability to learn, vivaciousness, sound body and the ability to cope well with the harshest conditions.

When town-dwelling people "discovered" the Puli around 1910, they also tried to make the breed more attractive to the eye. To begin with they tried to eliminate the obvious irregularities—bad coats, large bodies, chocolate brown colours, prick ears, etc. Then the experts took over.

When buying a Puli, do not choose one only because he looks attractive. The present qualities of the Puli were achieved by conserving all its valued characteristics, except the length of the coat. Heavy thick fringes on the head which cover the eyes can become troublesome. The same is true of the hair on the trunk and on the limbs which sometimes reaches the ground, or is even longer. It may look attractive but it certainly obstructs the Puli in his movement. We cannot aim at breeding two different types for the length of the hair, but will have to concentrate on shortening the hair of the working dogs. While the dogs are actually working, the natural wear and tear will stop the coat from growing too long.

The essence of *breeding by ancestry* is that the puppy inherits its characteristics from his parents, who had inherited theirs from their parents and so on. Pedigree experts, when explaining the good qualities of a particular Puli, like to mention certain outstandingly excellent ancestors regardless of how distant they were. If an excellent ancestor is seen to produce a line of high quality offspring, his influence becomes significant and we may wish to line breed to maintain and improve the virtues we have. In the last 30 to 40 years carefully planned breeding resulted in several successful lines and by combining these lines further inbreeding can now be avoided while the breed becomes more stable.

Selection by offspring. The acceptance of the principle that dogs can only be used for breeding after the offspring they produced had been carefully evaluated gave rise to great improvement.

Examination and selection of the offspring is carried out as follows:

The examination starts by pre-selection. This means that every Puli is first judged at a show or inspected at a stockbreeders' meeting. By checking the pedigree, each dog has its ancestry defined. The ancestry will not have to be presented on a separate document later in the proceedings. It is decided during

I Seven-week-old white Puli puppies

II Cream Puli bitch with black and cream puppies

III White Puli bitch, with corded coat

IV Black Puli bitch with an ideal coat
V Well-cared for, eight-year-old black Puli male, with a ribbon-type coat
VI Puli male with a well-proportioned head, one-and-a-half-year-old, black

VII Pumi's ideal coat   VIII Pumis have great vitality
IX Tough and agile: the Mudi

X Black Mudi with no markings

the examination whether the Puli is up to standard, in which case he or she can be used for breeding without restrictions. If he or she falls below the standard, breeding is strictly forbidden. Males must be more carefully appraised because they can produce more offspring than bitches. Each dog used in breeding is "re-evaluated" every year on the basis of the results his offspring achieved during the previous year. Dogs that have produced many high quality puppies are widely recommended for further stud work.

Uniformity of the breed, together with the more attractive appearance which has been achieved in the last few years, is partly due to this method of examining the offspring.

Preparation for breeding. Pulis usually reach sexual maturity at the age of nine months, but this does not mean that they are mature enough to be bred. If used for breeding when too young, their later development, their health or even the quality of their first litter may suffer. Pulis have reached maturity for breeding when they can be bred without endangering their own development, bitches arrive at this stage at the age of 16 months, dogs at 24. Only very well developed dogs should be bred earlier.

Management and housing. Pulis have always been hardy dogs. Softer animals could not put up with the rough living conditions of the Puszta, as the shepherds did not pay special attention to how their dogs were housed. The Puli's natural instinct always enabled it to find protection for itself. Owing to the good thermal insulation of its coat, particularly the fine underwool, only very cold winter storms would drive it to shelter. Survival was only possible for hardy dogs with tough and sound bodies.

Town-dwelling people find it difficult to understand why Pulis sometimes prefer the bare ground to their kennel or place in the house, even during cold winters. The Puli's past, the living conditions its ancestors knew explains this. Pulis choose the cold ground instead of warm blankets if it means freedom of movement and better opportunities of keeping an eye on what is going on around them.

To house a Puli one can use a kennel or just a simple packing case. The most important points to remember are to shelter the Puli from the wind and provide it with a dry resting place where rain cannot reach it. When deciding the size of its kennel we shall have to take into account whether it will house only a working dog or whether it will also be used breeding.

A kennel housing one dog should be 50 cm wide, 70 cm deep and 70 cm high. A kennel for a Puli used for breeding should measure 80 cm wide, 110 cm deep and 70 cm high. The walls should be made of wood or brick. The floor also must be of wood or insulated bricks, or even plastic tiles. It is useful if the roof can be removed. There is no need to put blankets on the floor because Pulis do not require this kind of comfort even in winter. Blankets are difficult to keep clean and are excellent breeding spots for parasites. A small amount of straw during winter will insure the dog's perfect comfort. While the puppies are still feeding from the bitch they should be confined to the kennel. The sides of the packing case or the doorway of the kennel will stop them wandering away. A few weeks later a piece of wood should be placed at the entrance as a ramp to help the puppies climb in and out of the house.

A Puli should freely move around the house and garden with no restrictions at all. In some cases, though, its freedom must be limited to certain areas. Some people are reluctant to keep Pulis because they are afraid that the vegetables and flowers in their garden will be destroyed by a dog of such lively temperament. It is possible to protect the garden by putting up a small fence, some 40 cm high, near the main paths and to train the Puli not to cross it. Two rows of wire fixed at a height of 15 and 30 cm will serve the same purpose, and will be sufficient warning to trained dogs. Sometimes a Puli guarding a house or an entry is kept on a running chain. (This is a chain attached by a ring to a strong wire stretched between two trees or posts.) Kennel compound housing can be a last resort. A dog requires a kennel area of at least 4×5 m in size. The fence is best made of wire 1.5 m high. The open air section of the kennel run should provide both sunshine and shade.

Feeding. It is widely known how well a Puli can manage even with the worst living conditions. Shepherding and the vicissitudes of the life on the Puszta have accustomed him to this. The fact that he does not demand special feeding does not mean that he can be starved or should always be given the same kind of food. Lack of food leads to loss of energy and an unbalanced diet to various degenerative illnesses that are caused by a lack of vitamins and body building substances.

Pulis should be fed once a day, pregnant and lactating bitches twice daily.

The Puli's nutritional needs are the same as that of any medium sized vigorous dog.

Grooming. We have discussed the special grooming of the Puli's hair in a previous chapter. Here we would like to make a few more suggestions.

Puppies need no special grooming. They must be kept in a clean place and their coat refreshed by simple brushing and combing. They should not be bathed at all, because drying is difficult and can present serious problems (the puppy may catch cold and the coat will lose its natural oil).

When the puppy is 9 months old we can leave the hair to take its natural shape. By 9 months frequent brushing and combing must be stopped. If the hair is too fine we must be careful not to let it become felted. This process can be arrested by tearing up the hair and spinning it into cords, as previously described.

Parts of the body that get dirty easily (around the lips, anus, feet) can be frequently washed. A fully-grown Puli should be kept clean without bathing, if possible. Some Pulis really enjoy being cleaned with a vacuum cleaner. If bathing cannot be avoided, one has to be extremely careful not to upset the shape of the coat but try to squeeze the water out of the coat by gently patting it all over with a towel. The hair must be thoroughly dried after bathing, especially in winter, when the danger of the dog catching cold is greater.

Bitches and dogs must be carefully prepared for mating, as a thick coat of hair might be obstructive. Thick or matted hair will have to be cut off around the vulva. It might help if the tail of the bitch is tied up. Long hair must also be removed from around the dog's scrotum.

Judging Pulis

Selective breeding demands the earliest possible selection of the puppies, as it is easier to judge a puppy at 6–8 weeks old than at a later stage of development. When the puppy is 18 months to 2 years old it can be finally decided whether or not he should be used for breeding. One must be well-acquainted with principles of responsible selection, and the Puli's important characteristics.

The colour of the coat and its marks serve as the basis for the selection of *new-born puppies*. Black Pulis are born with glossy black hair. Grey Pulis are either born black and go grey later in life, or have a grey coat of hair at the moment of birth. White Pulis are born white, cream ones will become lighter in colour in the course of time.

Pigmentation and the colour of the hair can be judged at birth. The colour of the well-pigmented skin is slate grey. In some cases the colour might be a slightly lighter variation of grey, but soon after birth (by the time the puppy is 1–2 weeks old) it will become dark grey. If the skin is flesh coloured or has lighter spots the puppy should not be used in breeding.

The formation of the hair of a puppy few days old must be very carefully examined. The following formation can be found: astrakhan-like, curly; thick wavy; loose wavy, straight, long hair; straight short hair. The latter does not bear the characteristics of the breed and cannot be used in breeding. Puli puppies with long, straight hair will develop straight, open-haired coats, and must also be excluded from breeding. Puppies having any of the other formation of hair can be accepted. Astrakhan-like coats will probably be corded, the loose-wavy coats are most likely to become felted or wide-ribboned coats.

The stance, the shape of the body, the tail-carriage and the chances of development of a young puppy can be judged best before weaning.

The square shape of the body may already be observed. The muzzle tends to be slightly shorter in relation to the proportion of the skull as in later age. If this proportion equals the proportions of an adult dog, the nose might be longer than desired by the time the puppy is fully grown. The good tail-carriage of a very young Puli is not likely to deteriorate. Sickle-tails often take up the ideal position (when the tail is curled over the loins), at a later stage of development. Tail-carriage must be observed in different situations, and more than just once. (For example, while the puppy is eating or playing.) A well-developed young puppy will retain its natural vigour.

A *young Puli* does not show its adult shape but has an adolescent appearance. Its proportions are not yet fully developed. Its coat is only medium length, stiff or fluffy, teddy-bear like. This is one of the reasons why it is impossible to judge the potentials of a young Puli. An early opinion might lead to great disappointment, so it is much wiser to judge the Puli only when it is 18 months or 2 years old. In the meantime, we should provide it with plenty of exercise and unrestricted movement to help it to develop a healthy and sound body.

Judging an adult dog. It is necessary to prepare a Puli before taking it to a show, as they generally are not used to strangers. Besides grooming, preparation includes conditioning to crowds and handling by strangers, and lead training. It must be trained to walk on the left hand side of its handler. We must make sure that schooling does not result in unpleasant associations because if this happens, the Puli will be shy and will look frightened in the presence of a judge. It will let its tail drop, or pull it between its legs, will sulk and give an altogether disappointing impression.

Ideally, during an examination, the eyes of the judge should be at the same height as the Puli's body. This is nearly impossible to achieve. To place the Puli on a table might help, but because this situation may seem strange, the dog may be ill at ease. Judging a Puli while sitting down is a very good practice, or at least bending down often to get a full picture of the animal placed about 4–5 m away from the judge. Small platforms used at shows are becoming more and more popular, and the Puli may easily become accustomed to them.

The judging of movement must take place on even ground. The Puli should first be walked towards the judge on a straight course, and then directly away so that hind movement can be assessed at normal walking pace. Then the handler and dog will move in a circle around the judge at the trot, or faster. Later the dog is halted while the judge makes a more detailed examination. There are three ways to do this:

(1) To get a *general impression,* the judge has only to examine the most important parts of the body. The general impression forms the basis of the whole judgement.

(2) Classification: Here a more detailed analysis is needed to be able to decide in which class the shown animal should be placed. Within each class a ranking order can be established. This classification is also often the finishing touch when judging by points.

(3) The most accurate method is when *points* are given to show the standard of various qualities or a *detailed report* is written up on each Puli. These two methods may be combined or may be employed separately. When giving points to mark the quality of each separate part of the body and every characteristic of a Puli, the highest number of points is 100. A written report serves the same purpose, only it is a detailed document in words instead of numbers. These methods of judging a Puli take a long time, but are thorough and most helpful and accurate.

The Puli's work. No other breed can be compared to Pulis in herding. Their talents are best revealed when working sheep; Pulis are a great help in guarding the sheep in the fields or the sheep-fold, and at milking time will bring the sheep to the shepherd. It has been recorded that a ewe did not want to allow her lamb to feed and it was the Puli who kept the mother stationary until the lamb satisfied its appetite.

As fields became smaller, the Puli's duty was mainly to guard the estate and the house; nowadays more of them are carrying out these duties than fulfilling the task for which they were originally intended. The Puli keeps all strangers away from the house, for it has a volatile temperament, is always alert, and has a loud bark. If it has been trained to guard a house, it will attack fearlessly, with great courage, putting larger dogs to shame.

The self-respect and proud dignity of the Puli might be its only drawback. If it is punished or scolded when it thinks unjustified, it tends to sulk. It trots away unhappily, and sometimes keeps up its mood for as long as a day. If its master proves to be consistently just, there is no reason why the Puli should be easily offended.

Its lively temperament and unquestionable reliability enables it to be used for guarding goods in lorries and containers. It crouches without being noticed, and at the moment of danger leaps up barking loudly. Pulis are also successfully used for guarding private cars. A Puli would not desert the car it has been told to guard. Having got used to travelling by car, it can easily become addicted to it.

Pulis were trained by the police between the two world wars. Police-Pulis were known to have won several international competitions. Pulis are no longer used for police work, as the size of dog that was needed to do this job is not bred now.

Breeders have often wondered whether a smaller size Puli (under 31 cm) ought to be bred. The question has arisen, since many Pulis are kept nowadays in town houses and flats as pets. Such a Puli would be likely to lose some of its virtues and this should not be allowed to happen. It must retain the qualities necessary for the purpose for which it was bred. In former times sheep dogs were brought to town from the country by enthusiastic breeders. Now it is more common to find that thoroughbred improved Pulis are taken back to their rural environment where they are expected to resume their traditional role.

The Pumi

(Canis familiaris ovilis villosus terrarius Raitsitsi. Anghi, 1935*)*

Origin. The name "Pumi" is first mentioned in 1815, describing a kind of sheep dog. For a century the word "Pumi" was confused with the word "Puli". In certain parts of Hungary the name Pumi was more frequently used, while in others, Puli was more common. "Pumi" may have derived from "Puli". The breed emerged about the 17th or 18th century probably as a result of cross breeding German Spitz, French Briard sheep dogs, a variety of Terrier and Hungarian Puli. This cross breeding produced dogs whose coat was shorter and more wiry than that of the Puli, whose head was more elongated, who had semi-pricked ears, erect with the tips bent forward. These dogs had an unusually lively temperament and proved to be a great help in herding sheep and rounding up cattle (Drawing no. 1).

The Pumi in 1815

Experts in dog breeding noticed the century-old confusion between Pulis and Pumis. It was Raitsits who defined the real difference between the original type of Puli and the Pumi. The latter breed appeared long after Pulis became a separate breed. Raitsits also discovered that the basic differences can be further emphasized by careful breeding. Separate breeding of Pulis and Pumis started at the beginning of this century. Separation had a different effect on each of the two types. Pulis quickly became fashionable and were taken up by selective specialist breeders, while Pumis excelled as working dogs. The breeding of Pumis still requires a lot of skill and knowledge. Dogs bred in the country by shepherds are often more typical examples of this breed than any of the carefully bred pedigreed Pumis. The breed offers an interesting challenge to the enthusiastic student of canine hereditary traits. In 1921, while working on the standard description of the different Hungarian bred dogs, Raitsits suggested the need to consider Pumis as a separate breed. Pumis were classified as a regional variety of the Pulis at a show in 1920, while in 1923 they appear as an independent breed. The first outline for a standard description dates back to 1921. Entries in *The Pedigree Book of Hungarian Dogs* show how popular this breed became in the years following official recognition. In 1924 there were 265 entries for Komondors, 458 for Kuvasz, 255 for Pulis and 130 for Pumis (over half the number of Pulis entered). Dr. Csaba Anghi mentions that at a dog show in Budapest in 1927, out of 300 contestants there were 19 Komondors, 28 Kuvasz, 35 Pulis and 12 Pumis.

The separation of Pulis and Pumis took a long time to accomplish. Carefully planned selective breeding in the last 50 years is directed towards eliminating all overlapping characteristics of both breeds.

The Pumi and its Changing Role during its History

Old pictures testify that its characteristics have gone through basic changes. Its coat is the feature which most retains its original form. The ideal coat does not mat, the hair is medium length or shorter. The shape of the head was not uniform. There were Pumis with a pronounced stop and deep-set eyes, while others had a flat bridge to the nose and large eyes. All these variations could be found 50 years ago as well as today. The same confusion applies to the shape of the ears. From the early days the ideal shape, pricked ears with drooping points, occurred as well as small, pointed erect ears.

Raitsits called the Pumi "the sheep dog terrier", and pointed out that breeding should preserve all the outstanding useful features of the terrier blood.

Pumis are very active, lively and energetic, always alert and ready to work with cattle and pigs as well as sheep. Even now Pumis are mainly bred by herdsmen. A small number of Pumis live in villages or towns where they are trained to kill rodents or to protect property.

Standard Description

Today's valid standard description dates from 1960, and is filed as the No. 56/b standard. Its main purpose was to define a high standard for the breeding.

General impression. Pumis are medium sized sheep herding dogs with some terrier features. Any coat colour is acceptable, provided it is a solid colour and not broken by white markings. The coat is of medium length and does not mat. The skin must have dark pigmentation. The terrier ancestry appears most obvious in the shape of the head: the muzzle is longer than the Puli's, with a straight or nearly straight stop-line. The eyes are not covered and the ears are erect with drooping points. The neck joins the trunk at a steeper angle than on Pulis, and the dog should always look alert. Despite the long legs the body would fit into a square. Pumis are intelligent, lively, self-assertive and inclined to be noisy.

Description of the Parts of the Body

The head is oval, relatively narrow. Its shape is determined by the length of the head. The skull is of medium width and is slightly domed. The forehead is long and also slightly domed, but in profile it appears flat. The eyebrows are not very pronounced. The eyes are oval, dark brown and are set moderately oblique. The stop is not evident (especially on Pumis of the last few generations) since the forehead continues in an almost straight line to the straight muzzle. The nose is long and pointed. The nostrils are narrow. The cheeks are well muscled, the eyelids fit closely, showing no haw. The lips are also tightly set on the teeth.

The teeth are extremely strong and well developed. The ideal bite is the scissors bite. Overshot mouths are uncommon, and the lack of premolars is also rare.

The eyes, the muzzle and lips are visible, since long hair does not cover the head.

The ears are set high, they are V-shaped, erect and of medium size, with the points of the ears drooping forward. This drooping section makes up one-third of the whole of the leather but sometimes it is only the very point that bends. The ideal formation is when the point of the ear drops forward and slightly sideways. Ears that are set on the side of the head or are drawn backwards do not give the typical impression. Prick ears are not characteristic of the breed and show the intrusion of either Mudi or Spitz blood. The shape and angle of the ears indicate terrier ancestry and are very important features to be preserved.

The neck joins the trunk at a rather steep angle. It is of medium length, very strong, well arched and very mobile, enabling the Pumi to perform the rapid head turning movements so typical of the breed. A too short neck is not so agile, and an overlong neck often goes with a slack body.

The top line rises slightly over the withers, and slopes a little towards the back. The tail may correct the shape of the generally sloping croup.

Steep shoulder blades emphasize the prominent withers. Loins are of short or of medium length but always strong and muscular. The chest and the hindquarters are of medium width. The rib cage is flat and deep, with flanks slightly drawn up. The dog should be in hard condition but bitches who have had several litters tend to be flabby.

The tail is set high, and is either rolled over the loins or carried straight with the end curled up. Generally the tail is docked to 2/3 of the original length, putting more emphasis on the terrier-like appearance.

The forelimbs should be straight and rather long, not too wide apart, the pasterns form cca. 55° to the horizontal, and are steep. The feet are tight, the pads springy, and the nails very hard. Dew claws must be removed since they may hinder the Pumi's movement.

The hindlegs are set back from the body. The thighs are extremely long, while the hock is of moderate length.

36 Ideal Pumi dog

37 Four-week-old Pumi puppies
38 Curly-coated 18-month-old Pumi dog

39 Five-month-old Pumi puppy

40 Three-year-old Pumi dog

41 Pumi awaiting command
42 Grey Pumi dog, a longer coat or more hair on the head is objectionable
43 Pumi puppy while training
44 Pumis are also suitable for boar hunting

45 Mudi dog watching

46 Five-week-old Mudi puppies
47 Ideal, well-built Mudi dog with a pronounced stop

48 Mudis are not only excellent shepherds but also suitable as pets

49 Curly coated Mudi bitch with a very good head but too long body

The colour of *the skin* is slate grey and well pigmented. The hairless parts of the body are either slate grey or black. The colour of the eye should be dark brown or black.

Pigmentation tends to be perfect in most Pumis, parti-colouring of the skin is very rare. The colour of the eye, on the other hand, may deviate from brown. The colour might range from light brown to yellow, or even bluish. Light brown eyes are acceptable, but yellow or blue colouring is considered a serious fault and excludes a Pumi from breeding.

The coat of the Pumi is quite unique. It consists of a rough top coat and a finer undercoat in a 50–50 ratio. Compared to the Puli the Pumi coat is generally rougher but has more variations. The whole body is covered by shaggy rough fur. The preferred coat is the harsh type since that contains the least quantity of wooly undercoat. Longer plaited coats contain a higher percentage of fluffy hair but even those never felt or mat, not even on the hindquarters or thighs.

The hair is shortest on the paws and on the muzzle, so that the eyes and nose are always visible. Bushy, wiry hair covers the ears. The hair on the neck, trunk, limbs and tail can vary between 3–4 cm, or 5–7 cm. When a Pumi's coat is longer than desired it may resemble the coat of a poorly furred Puli, but even then there are still differences in length and texture. Some bitches shed their entire coat at whelping, while others may lose only part of the coat.

There are many variations of coat colour. Any colour is acceptable as long as it is a whole colour. Parti-colouring, or coats with broken markings do not meet the requirement of the standard.

The most common colours are: silver grey, light grey, slate grey, grizzle, rusty brown, faded black, white and pale sandy-yellow. The two rarest colours are pure white or black. No coat should have different coloured patches intermixed with the dominant colour. Puppies are normally born black, but by the time they are weaned the final, lighter colour has appeared. The puppies start shedding their puppy coat around the lips and the eyes. The new hair will be a lighter greyish colour. Puppies at this stage of growth look rather odd.

Movement. The Pumi's movement is lively and gay, the gait short and brisk. Pumis are inexhaustible, always busy and active.

Breed Characteristics. Dogs of this breed do not have a consistently uniform appearance, due mainly to the relatively recent separation of the Pumis from the Pulis, and the not yet fully established standard. Despite the efforts of selective breeding, Pumis are still being born which do not conform to the standard. To achieve better results it is very important to remember that Pumis are not just Pulis with bad coats, but an entirely different breed with many different characteristics. Pulis are long haired sheep dogs while *Pumis are herding terriers with medium long coats.*

Terrier characteristics are an essential part of Pumi features. This applies to outward appearance and temperament. The terrier-look is given by the nearly angular shape of the head, the straight stopline, the erect ears with their drooping tip and the high-set tail. A very lively temperament, the sharp bark, the excellent sense of smell and the passion for rat hunting are also terrier characteristics.

Sex differences are not easily noticeable because of the lack of uniformity in the breed. Dogs may have a relatively delicate build, while some bitches may be more robust. The aim of present and future selective breeding is to make the secondary sexual characteristics more definite.

Proportions. Pumis, on the whole, are well proportioned and attractive to the eye. Although the body seems to be square the legs look longer than average. In England they say such dogs are weedy. The rib cage appears to be flat because of the Pumi's shorter hair. The head also seems to be slightly too large, but only because one automatically compares the Pumi's proportions to that of the Puli's. If one compares the Pumi to terriers, the vivacity that governs the Pumi's every movement immediately becomes obvious. The Pumi's stance and the alert watching position greatly improves its appearance.

Body measurements. Pumis are medium size dogs. The ideal height of the withers by a measuring stick is 35 to 44 cm.

The measurements of the different sections of the body given as a percentage of the height at the withers are:

	minimum	ideal
length of the trunk	100%	100
depth of the chest	43%	45
width across chest from withers to withers	30%	33
around the trunk	115%	120
length of the head	44%	45
the length of the muzzle as percentage of the length of the head	45%	–

Weight: 8 to 13 kg.

Puppies appear to be delicate because of their fine bone structure and taut muscle but one can tell by running the hands over them how well developed and tough Pumis are.

Weight of puppies at different stages of development.

The average weight of puppies while on the dam, in grams.

At birth	1	2	3	4	5	6	7
	\multicolumn{7}{c}{months}
190–240	350–400	500–700	800–950	1100–1400	1450–1900	1950–2500	2400–3500

The average weight of puppies after weaning, in kgs.

3	4	5	6	9	12
months					
3.5–5.0	4.2–6.5	4.7–7.5	5.5–8.0	5.8–8.5	6.1–9.0

Their size was determined by the work they have done generation after generation. If their body was any larger they would not be so hardy; on the other hand, a smaller dog would find it difficult to control large animals.

Condition. Pumis are never fat, they only gain weight in old age. They should be hard and lean, even tending to look thin and gaunt. Pumis should be presented at shows in good condition carrying a little more weight than the working dog, since it makes them look more attractive.

Temperament. Pumis are very lively, even more active than Pulis, but more responsive than Fox Terriers. Pumis not only use their noses and register everything that goes on around them, but also give tongue. They always appear busy, investigating every noise and scent, and commenting with a sharp bark. The commands of his master, a nod or direction by the eyes evokes a short bark from the Pumi as if he were holding a conversation with his master.

Pumis are intelligent and adaptable. Despite their fiery temperament they become very pleasant companions if enough attention is paid to them. Their *ability to learn* is quite surprising, from puppy days they copy their mother or the other dogs around them, naturally and without any special effort. If Pumis are submitted to specialized training there is no limit to their capabilities. Most well-trained Pumis show off their knowledge with enthusiasm and pleasure. Herding Pumis work with great concentration. Pumis are extremely hardy dogs and can easily put up with the worst weather or poor food. This is the result of the survival of the fittest, for the shepherd never paid attention to nursing sick animals. The shepherds wormed their dogs with the remedies nature had to offer, the rest was left to the Pumi's sound body and high level of resistance.

Type. Pumis are sheep dogs with terrier characteristics. Their temperament, physical structure and appearance, their behaviour and activities all show this. If a shepherd or a professional breeder has ever worked with Pumis he is unlikely to want another breed. The only undesirable feature may be the loud bark, which can prove a drawback in certain situations, unless the dog is taught and trained when to use it. If this constant "conversation" is not enjoyed, another, similar type of dog should be kept. On the other hand the short coat is a great advantage, as it means that Pumis can be kept in town houses, too. The breed is becoming more and more popular each year.

Breeding Pumis. Breeding Pumis requires more attention than breeding either Pulis or Komondors, because their breed characteristics are not yet fully established. The fact, that the studbook for Pumis is still open is an advantage on one hand, while a drawback on the other. Typical Pumis coming from the country where they have been raised by the shepherds are always welcome in selective breeding kennels, since they refresh the blood lines. At the same time, because their ancestry is unknown, unpleasant surprises might be in store for the breeder when the new generation of puppies arrives. If a Pumi is exported to a foreign country, his ancestry must be definitively documented down to the great-grandparents. Working Pumis, or the puppies of working Pumis, will always be favoured for breeding. They respond to either the usual working training, or its elementary form (training in behaviour). Behaviour training includes: how to behave in the street, at dog shows, and as companion dog around the house.

Pumis should never be turned into useless pets. The ability to learn and to be trained is strongly hereditary. Individuals that lack this quality should not be used for breeding, even if they are attractive to the eye.

Pumis with good bodily conformation and correct temperament are greatly valued since the breed characteristics are still in need of strengthening.

It often happens when breeding Pumis that even though one parent may be of poor quality, with a well chosen partner, excellent puppies can be produced. This method, since it is unreliable, should not be made the basis for future breeding, it is more fruitful to try to mate only high quality couples. At present the second generation of selectively bred puppies are being born, and the result is encouraging. There are quite a large number of these "new" Pumis, so a definite homogeneous line can be anticipated after another two generations.

It would be a mistake to be too definite about the right age for breeding. A good bitch can start breeding once she is over one year old. The same age limit applies to dogs. We consider this relatively early start for breeding useful, since we are then able to determine the quality of the first, early litter and decide the genetic value of the parents. The bitch should be taken to the dog. If a working bitch is to be mated, she may be nervous away from home because of the strange environment. Very severe reactions have been known, when the bitch has been so terrified that for days she stays in the same, transfixed position. This is the time when her master's kind words and understanding are essential. Bitches should be allowed some time to get used to their partners, instead of being abruptly introduced and force-mated.

Housing Pumis. Pumis are hardy dogs, so housing should present no problems. Though their coat is not long, the upper hair and the undercoat make an excellent insulator, and they easily withstand the worst weather. They dry quickly and have no objection to working in muddy fields.

If Pumis live as household pets they should have a kennel as their resting place. The same size should be used for Pumis as for Pulis. Pumis can even be kept in flats, as they are easy to keep clean, they pick up less dust and dirt than long coated dogs. Pumis become more and more popular as town dogs, as they are so companionable, and they can be trained not to bark in an urban environment. Pumis should present no problem for the housewife. We know some Pumis who are trained to sit outside the front door until their paws are washed and dried before coming indoor after a walk. Kennelled dogs become bored and will inevitably be more noisy.

Feeding. Pumis are even less fussy feeders than Pulis. Special attention should be paid to diet in the first nine months of their lives, later on they will do well on the most basic feeding regime. Pumi puppies are fed in the way already described for Pulis, but they may need a little more food, as they are so energetic.

Grooming the Pumi is much simpler than grooming the long haired sheep dogs. Dead hair is shed and does not stay in the coat. If this is helped by thorough brushing once a week, the Pumi will look well groomed. The natural orifices of the body can be kept clean by wiping them with a damp sponge.

Frequent bathing is not recommended, unless the Pumi lives completely indoors, in which case he can be bathed once a fortnight. Puppies should not be bathed until they are over 4 months old.

Judging Pumis

One must remember that the breed is still in the process of being established, so Pumis not showing definite breed characteristics must be strictly excluded from future breeding. Mouths normally present no problems, nor does coat colour. If the hair is either too short, too long or straight, the Pumi should not be used for breeding.

The main requirements are: the head showing terrier features, pricked ears with drooping points, dark brown eyes, high and straight tail carriage, and a lively temperament. These characteristics are essential in every dog.

Unweaned puppies do not show all their future quality, they look more like Pulis with a pointed nose. By the time the puppies are weaned the difference between the breeds begins to be obvious. Puppies at the age of 4–5 months already give definite signs of their breed characteristics but at this age one still cannot form a final opinion of the shape of the head and the posture of the ears. Blunt, coarse heads may refine and become terrier-like later on. Pumis with perfectly shaped ears may lose them because the points of the ears straighten up. Head conformation cannot be judged until the puppy is over 9 months, neither can temperament.

The Pumi's *work* is diverse nowadays. Pumis are almost the only breed that can be used for herding as well as guarding homes, or as companions in the home with the same success.

Their versatility is enormous but the majority are still working cattle and sheep dogs.

Pumis who are house dogs are the living burglar alarm of the household. They are interested in everything, nothing escapes their attention and they like to be involved with everything that goes on around them, thus providing more security than heavy locks and bolts. Their method of guarding the house is totally different to that of Komondors or the Kuvasz. The Pumi's main principle is prevention, all irregular attempts at entry are nipped in the bud.

Pumis are used for killing rats, too, with very good results. As they have an excellent sense of smell, great energy, a tight grip, and are eager and fearless in attack, it might prove worthwhile to train more Pumis for boar hunting.

Pumis have been kept in towns for 50 years but fortunately this has so far not divided the breed into working dogs and useless pets. Pumis who have lived in urban surroundings all their lives can become herding dogs in a very short time once taken back to their original environment. The contrary can also easily happen, puppies raised by shepherds can turn into town dogs.

These two different ways of life blend easily nowadays, without any damaging effect on each other's existence. This is to the advantage of the Pumi, since better living improves their attractive looks without detracting from their eagerness to learn and their hardy physique.

The Mudi *(Canis ovilis Fényesi.* Anghi, 1936.*)*

The origin of this breed dates back to the end of the 19th century, or the beginning of the 20th. When zoologists separated Pulis and Pumis as individual breeds, they discovered the existence of a third type of sheep dog. This breed can be found in all parts of Hungary.

The third variety sheep dog was first described by Mr. Dezső Fényesi who was the director of the local museum in the small town of Balassagyarmat. He was the first enthusiast to organize selective breeding of this type of sheep dog which he called Mudi.

Mudis are bred largely by shepherds and herdsmen. There are only very few pure, hobby breeders dedicated to raising Mudis, so the number of Mudis bred by them is very low.

Standard Description

General impression. Mudis are medium size herding sheep dogs. Their coat is the shortest of all Hungarian sheep dogs. The limbs and the paws are almost smooth, while the rest of the body is covered by 3–4 cm long hair. This hair can either be wavy, or curly. Mudis have lively temperaments. The head is long and tapering with pointed prick ears. The tail is carried down. The shape of the body is rectangular, the top line sloping towards the hindquarters. Coat colour can be black, white or parti-coloured.

Description of the Parts of the Body

The head is oval, with a slightly arched dome. The forehead looks finely curved in profile, the stop is almost negligible. The eyebrows are slightly emphasized, the muzzle is narrow and pointed. The eyes are oval, dark brown and slightly oblique. The nostrils are narrow. The eyelids and the lips fit tightly. Teeth should be even with scissors bite.

The erect open prick ears are set high on the head and are very mobile. The neck is medium long, slightly arched, very muscular, set at an angle of 50–55° with the body. There should be no excessive hair or fold of skin on the neck.

The upper line of the body slopes slightly towards the croup. Low set hindquarters emphasize this sloping line. The rib cage is rounded and long, the back short and straight. The loins are medium length and well supported by muscles. The croup is short and rather flat. The tail is set and carried low, usually docked to 2–3 cm long. If a puppy is born with a short tail, this is not regarded as a fault. The ribs are well sprung, flanks slightly tucked up. Both testicles must be descended into the scrotum.

Forelimbs. The shoulderblades are sloping. The forearm is medium length, straight with tight elbows. The shoulder is well laid back. The pasterns are straight. The feet are tight with arched toes and thick pads.

Hindquarters. The croup falls away slightly, emphasized by the low set tail. The second thigh is long and well muscled, with short pasterns. The whole hindquarters is well angulated and powerful, set rather far back from the body. Dew claws should be removed.

The colour of *the skin* is dark slate grey and contains plenty of pigment. The hairless parts of the body are always black, and never parti-coloured or showing lack of pigmentation. The nails are slate grey. The colour of the skin in always dark even underneath light hair.

The hair is short, and glossy on the head, the front of the limbs and on the paws. The hair on the ears is long and wiry. The rest of the body is covered in thick, very wavy or curly, glossy hair that is 3–7 cm long. This type of hair never mats or gets tangled. The locks of hair form separate whirls and lines. The hair is longest on the elbows and on the thighs, where it forms "flags".

The coat can be black, black-and-white, or white-and-black with scattered patches, or white. The paws are the same colour as the rest of the coat.

The Mudi's *movement* is always lively and quick. His trotting action is short, but his gallop is longer and more ranging.

Breed Characteristics. There are different regional varieties, since Mudis are not yet closely bred. All versions are alike in the following features: short hair, pointed prick ears, straight or drooping tail, oval head, lively temperament and herding ability.

Mudis are different from Pulis or Pumis, and this difference emphasizes the Mudi's own, individual character. The appearance of the male is not vastly different from the bitch.

Mudis are well proportioned, somewhat long bodied dogs, active, tough, determined and vigorous. They are suitable to keep in towns and flats as pets, as they are very attractive to look at, but they also make excellent guarding, herding sheep dogs.

Their bodily *proportions* can be best expressed as in relation to the height of the withers.

The measurements of the different sections of the body given as a percentage of the height of the withers:

the length of the trunk		103
depth of the rib cage		40
width of the rib cage		30
round the body		105
length of the head		42
length of nose	is	40% of the length of the head
length of ears	is	45% of the length of the head

Weight: 8–13 kgs.

Mudis are hardy dogs who can be maintained in good condition on the bare essentials of nutrition. Their temperament is lively, though Mudis are not as noisy as Pumis. They have great natural intelligence. Mudis are ready to *learn* and can be easily trained. They are exceedingly healthy and have a high level of disease resistance. Mudis have strong and sound physiques.

Breeding Mudis. The studbook for pedigree dogs is still open. More Mudis should be selectively bred, since the number of pure bred Mudis is very low. Mudis which have been raised by shepherds in rural areas need careful examination for breed characteristics. Less than perfectly coated individuals should not be used for breeding. Mudis with long hair, or Puli-shaped falls of hair on the head, with lack of pigmentation of the nose or pendent ears cannot be given pedigrees. Individuals with light brown or yellow eyes, or where the hair on the ears is short and smooth, or where there is no flag-like formation of the hair on the limbs, should not be used for breeding. Mudis either too long or too short in the body also fail the breed standard requirement.

Housing and feeding is the same as for Pulis and Pumis.

Grooming is easy and simple. The shiny, rather harsh coat can easily be kept clean if the dog is brushed and bathed frequently.

Judging Mudis

Puppies must be *judged* according to the standard description from an early age. The heads of unweaned Mudi puppies are more pointed and more narrow than Pumi puppies'. Their coat is also shorter. This characteristic will become more pronounced as the puppy gets older. The Mudi enjoys an outing and is a natural showman.

Their work. It is important to find a situation where their eagerness and lively temperament can be given a fair trial.

At any dog show there may be only a couple of Mudis competing which means that judging strictly according to the standard is difficult. Our aim is to get as many Mudis as possible into show breeding, and encourage the shepherds to bring their dogs to town.

We recommend Mudis either as kennel dogs or house pets to all those people who are attracted to this breed.

B) GUARDING SHEEP DOGS

The Kuvasz *(Canis familiaris undulans hungaricus.* Abonyi, 1935)

Origin

Kuvasz, like other types of Hungarian sheep dogs, were first used by the nomadic shepherds of the early Hungarians, because they needed large, brave and daring dogs to protect them and their herds against thieves and wild animals. This need could be called the creative force that produced the Komondor and the Kuvasz.

The reason these two breeds, similar in use, could survive without inter-breeding, is never going to be answered. Was it made possible by physical or regional differences, or was it due to selection and to special methods of animal raising of the different nomadic communities? One can only guess. The ancient and independent origin of the two breeds is proved by the entirely different line of ancestors, the strong genetic transmission of the special features and the inherited characteristics of both breeds. There is no doubt that the two breeds are entirely separate. There were lots of misconceptions during the 18th and 19th centuries all originating from the similar use of the two breeds. The shepherds did not have standard descriptions, they did not even register their dogs, but bred them with a practical aim in mind.

The Kuvasz is not such a unique breed as Komondors and Pulis are. Related breeds, meant for the same kind of work, can be found all over the world, from Tibet to Spain, wherever there is space for large herds of animals to live together (herds of sheep, horses, or cattle). Similar breeds to the Kuvasz are: the Tibetian Mastiff, the Mongolian sheep dog, the Tartar sheep dog, the Caucasian mountain dog, the Portuguese mountain dog and also the Albanian sheep dog. The colour of the hair is either yellowish-white or cream coloured. The Bouvier des Flandres, the sheep dog of the Pyrenees and the Maremann look so much like the Kuvasz that they could easily be taken for each other by a non-expert. The Slovakian Chuvach, the Polish Owczarek Podhalanski are considered to be of the same origin as the Kuvasz and the three breeds were only separated quite recently.

Historical documents throw little light on these breeds, mainly due to the fact that these dogs were often given similar names in earlier times.

Written documents from the 1600s already mention the Kuvasz as an individual breed. The first illustration of the Kuvasz and the Komondor as separate breeds can be found in Ferenc Pethe's* *Természethistória és mesterségtudomány* (Natural History and Professional Sciences) in 1815 (See Fig. II). Treitschke** has a drawing of a Kuvasz in his book, published in 1840: *Der ungarische steppige Schäferhund, Canis familiaris pannonicus (var. "A" hirsutus)*, as he calls them.

It is quite likely that the Kuvasz was known to the Hungarians at the time of the Great Migration. Some historians believe that the Kuvasz breed was first used by the Hungarian shepherds after the Cuman assimilation (13th century). During the reign of King Matthias (1458–1490), Kuvasz were regularly used at big hunts, and noblemen often exchanged well-bred Kuvasz as presents.

At the time of the Turkish rule (16th–17th century) a similar, Turkish sheep dog blood-line might have been introduced but ever since the 17th century the breed kept its characteristics unchanged.

Original use and changes in use. The chief enemies of the nomadic shepherd were the wolves and thieves. The herds had to be protected from these intruders, but the shepherd could not do this job alone. Since the wolves normally attacked at night the best colour for the dog was white or very light cream, so that the shepherds could always tell their dogs from the wolves. Every guarding sheep dog all over the world happens to be white or very light coloured, which seems to support this theory. To carry out his work, a Kuvasz needed a good sense of smell, powerful teeth, eagerness in attack, never fading courage and, above all, steel-like muscles. Shepherds fed their dogs mainly on meat. A piece of meat was tied to a pole just high enough for the puppies to reach it, so the young Kuvasz could exercise their teeth and the muscles of the neck, the back and the limbs while mauling the meat to pieces.

The shape of the body, the attractive, lean structure of the Kuvasz is explained by the hard work required of them all through the centuries. They had to win the fight with the wolf, so they had to excell their enemy in agility and speed. When intensive farming replaced the old nomadic way of life, when swamps were drained and the shepherds raising live-stock in the open plains had to employ more sophisticated methods, the Kuvasz lost his original type of work. He lost most of his territory, and had to live and work near country houses, and later on, in villages just guarding property.

The Kuvasz shared a fairly isolated life with the shepherd, but this way of life kept the breed distinct and gave his existence purpose and aim. The breed could be kept pure by isolation but the danger of interbreeding was very great when the Kuvasz took up domestic life.

Registered, purposeful breeding started in 1905. This was the year when the Standard Description of the Hungarian Sheep Dogs was compiled. This standard was greatly improved by Professor Raitsits in 1921.

---

* Ferenc Pethe (1762–1832), author on economy and zoology
** Friedrich Treitschke (1776–1842), natural scientist

Drawing from 1815 of a Kuvasz, notice the short-haired head

The Abonyi*-Anghi**-Márki*** standard dates back to 1935, and served as the basis of selective breeding for a long time. The following years saw a great revival of interest in breeding Kuvasz. The breed became well known in Hungary and abroad, too. Kuvasz were exported to Holland, Switzerland and the USA. In Rumania, Czechoslovakia and in Poland similar breeding started with Kuvasz or their own variation of the breed.

The worst loss the breed suffered came with World War II when nearly the whole breed was destroyed. Only a few of these brave and daring dogs survived the storm of the war. Breeders and dog lovers searched the country for the few surviving Kuvasz and started breeding again. Thanks to this devoted work, the number of Kuvasz is rising steadily. At the present annual dog shows the usual number of Kuvasz entries is between 150–180.

Standard Description

The first standard description was written in 1905, followed by many others. The latest, revised version was completed in 1960. This standard was accepted by the FCI in 1963. Some extra details were added to this description in 1966, which has brought it up to date. The standard's catalogue number is FCI no 54/b.

Strict discrimination is needed to make the breed even more uniform and to conserve its present qualities—which this latest description hopes to define.

* Lajos Abonyi, veterinary surgeon, expert in dog breeding, at present the Vice President of the National Association of Hungarian Dog Breeders.
** Dr. Csaba Anghi (d. 1983), professor, ex-director of the Budapest Zoo, author of many books on animal breeding, Honorary President of the National Association of Hungarian Dog Breeders.
*** Iván Márki, veterinary surgeon, expert on breeding dogs, international judge at dog shows.

General impression. Kuvasz are big, strong working dogs with an average height of 70 cm. Their attractive, well balanced shape indicates strength and courage. They are well boned, but should not be coarse; well muscled with lean sinewy joints. The well-proportioned clean head and the almond shaped eyes indicate intelligence and loyalty. The deep chest and soundly constructed limbs, the slightly sloping topline provide the Kuvasz remarkable agility. The body must not be weedy nor cobly; seen from the side its rump is slightly longer than high. The middle line on the forehead is well defined. The eyelids and the lips are tight. The large teeth and the wide jaw muscles were developed by the constant fights Kuvasz were engaged in through the centuries. Around the neck they have a collar of profuse hair and on the back of the smooth-haired limbs the hair is longer.

Coat colour is white. The hair wavy and thick, a real characteristic of the breed. The skin has dark pigmentation. The gait is well-balanced, covering the ground well at the trot. The bark is deep and resonant.

The Kuvasz has an excellent sense of smell, and is highly intelligent, easily trained for guard duties. Kuvasz are loyal, but reserved in manner. Their attack is always dangerous, and unfair treatment may make them ferocious and uncontrollable.

Description of the Parts of the Body

The head. Although the whole dog is pleasing and well balanced, the most attractive part is the head. This is the Kuvasz' most distinctive feature, which makes him superior to all the other related breeds.

The shape of the head seen from above: the skull and the facial part of the head forms an angle of 45°. The skull is long and medium wide between the ears, tapering evenly towards the well-developed muzzle. The length of the head is important since it is only of moderate width. The muzzle narrows towards the nose without becoming pointed.

In profile the skull is only moderately arched—rather flat, continuing with a smooth line to a hardly perceptible stop and a long, straight nose. The middle line on the forehead is a finely carved groove, not too deep. The eyebrows are arched but not protruding. The eyes are medium size, slightly oblique, almond-shaped. The muzzle is straight. The face is covered by short hair. The cheek muscles are well developed but not too wide. The muzzle is not too deep, but not shallow either; of medium length, strong and well muscled.

From the front, the skull is prominent. Its base is wide, getting narrower towards the nose. The eyes must not be horizontal but set obliquely with tight rims. The head gives the impression of being lean. Males have larger and stronger heads, but never overlaid with muscles or fat, while bitches have finer bone structure. The head narrows to the nose, which is not thick or blunt, but the nostrils are wide. The lips do not droop, but close tight. Slack eyelids and drooping lips are bad hereditary faults. The corners of the mouth are serrated.

The *teeth* are strong, regular and well developed, closing in scissor bite. If the teeth close like pinchers the grip is not strong enough, so it must be considered a fault. The lower canine is in front of the upper one, both large and well developed.

The *eyes* are either dark brown or black. The eyelids are black. Their expression reflects strength and courage.

The *ears* are set high on the head. The upper third of the ears slightly stand away from the head but the rest of the leather droops close to the cheeks. They have the shape of a rounded V, and are slightly fleshy. When the dog is alert and watching, the ears may move a little but they are never pricked, nor is a Kuvasz able to perk up his ears. The ears are medium size, neither crinkled or flying.

The *neck* is medium long, thick, with strong muscles. It forms an angle of 30–40° to the horizontal. The head is strongly set on the muscular neck, the neck continuing to the shoulders and the brisket. The muscular neck was very important when Kuvasz were used for guarding herds. Often the neck was protected from wolf bites by a collar that had nails protruding from it. There is no loose skin on the neck, only a thick extra hair, a "collar". This may be very pronounced on males.

When describing *the upper line of the body* we talk about the continuous line that is formed by the withers, the back, the loin and the hindquarters, based on the firm, slightly sloping backbone. The withers rise over the line of the back, they continue to the neck at a slightly steep angle. The line of the trunk is unbroken from neck to withers, sometimes it is even difficult to tell where the actual joining occurs. The withers are only noticeable on poorly muscled individuals.

The ideal shape is: long withers, medium long back, short loins and medium long, slightly dipped croup. This shape was created by the Kuvasz' work which demanded sustained trotting.

The long withers, the medium long back together guarantee a long rib cage, medium wide and well sprung.

The *back* is straight. Bitches who have many litters may have sunken backs, so may heavily pregnant bitches. In every other case it is a sign of a slack physique, which excludes a Kuvasz from breeding.

The firm and short loins form a sound bridge between the front and the hindquarters. When he sheds his coat the thick hair on the hindquarters falls after the rest of the body coat, making the hindquarters seem to look out of proportion.

If the set of the hindlegs is correct the croup appears to be slightly flat.

The *belly* droops on bitches who already have had many litters, or on pregnant bitches. Usually, the belly is slightly tucked up.

The *tail* is carried low, and is a direct continuation of the sloping croup, reaching down to the hocks, with the tip slightly bending upwards but never curling. If a Kuvasz is excited or is moving in a fast trot, the tail may rise to the level of the loin, but not over it. Any other posture of the tail must be considered a fault. Cryptorchids are very rare, and may not be used in breeding.

The straight *front limbs* give the body firm support. Most Kuvasz have straight front limbs of medium length. Narrow fronts and long legs, or wide fronts and short legs are equally faulty. The front legs have approximately the same length as is the depth of the chest. The relatively deep chest ensures a strong support for the shoulder blades. It is very important to have strong ligaments and muscles joining the shoulder blades to the chest. If the muscles are weak the shoulder blades will be too high, giving a weak dog with slack movement.

An important requirement of the standard is for the pasterns to be steeper than 70°. Straight pasterns result in a mincing gait.

The *hindlegs* are much steeper and straighter than those of the German Shepherd Dogs. The pelvis forms approximately 90° to the thigh-bone, the stifles are at an angle of about 110 to 120° and the hocks at 130 to 140°. These ideal angles can be measured in relation to the vertically standing pasterns. Steep hindlegs shorten the step even though it makes the Kuvasz to be taller than his actual height. Animals with poor angulation get tired more easily since the stifles have to be stretched too much.

The *feet* are round and tight. The hind feet are oval shaped, while the front feet are rounder. Loose feet or splayfoot indicate a weak structure. The pads are full and springy. The pads are dark, grey, the nails slate grey. Dew claws should be removed.

All the limbs are lean. Kuvasz of sound construction have a strong healthy physique. This should be demanded of every individual of the breed. The gait should be free and smooth.

The *skin* contains a lot of pigment, and is slate grey. The nose, the eyelids and the lips are always black. It can happen—as a result of illness, or lack of adequate nourishment, in lactating bitches, or in very cold winter time—that the nose becomes 'pink'. This fading may be quite extensive, but naturally a constant dark pigmentation of the skin is more desirable. Such occasional lighter colour, if after a short while the Kuvasz regains his original, deep pigmentation, can not be classified as faulty. On the other hand, flesh coloured spots or complete lack of pigment are serious faults. The palate is also dark. Though parti-colouring can be tolerated here, it should not spread onto the lips.

The tongue of a healthy Kuvasz is bright red.

The colour of the skin under the hair is also slate grey, best seen on the belly, where the hair is less thick than on the rest of the body. Slight parti-colouring on the skin of the belly can be tolerated.

The *coat* of a Kuvasz is very attractive, and for the sake of the breed great attention must be paid to the coat when judging. The head is covered by short, straight, flat hair, as are the ears, the fore limbs and the hind legs. The hair on the head is short up to the nape. Longer hair is not desirable between the ears, or on the head, indeed it makes a Kuvasz look less attractive. The body, the upper part of the limbs, the neck and the tail are covered by thick, wavy, rather rough hair which forms whirls and waves and crests. Under the rougher upper hair finer undercoat can be found, the amount changing according to the seasons of the year.

The hair on the neck—mainly on the sides and the lower half of the neck—carries an abundant ruff, especially on males. This collar sometimes reaches down to the chest, forming a mane. The limbs are fringed down to the pasterns. The fringes are normally 5–7 cm long, or even longer on the thighs. The whole tail is covered with thick hair. The longest hair at the slightly curved-up tip of the tail, where it is 10–15 cm long, forms an attractive "flag".

The hair of a Kuvasz never forms cords and never mats. It may become heavy and thick on the hindquarters on an ungroomed dog. Straight hair on the trunk is not characteristic to the breed, and tight curls are attractive but undesirable. Slight curl of the mane is acceptable.

Coat colour. White is the colour of this breed, but many shades of white are known. Old documents mention pale, sandy, grizzly, or even black coated Kuvasz, and the whole range of colours do exist in the related breeds, too, but none with parti-coloured or spotted coats.

In Hungary even the first standard description requires a white coat; shepherds favoured the white colour in breeding too, since this easily distinguishable colour helped them in their work. Two variations of white are known: pure white and ivory. Both colours can be accepted, but the ears and the back should never show cream colouring. (Occasionally a temporary discolouring can be observed when a slight reddening of the skin and hair changes the real colour of the Kuvasz. These dogs have extra sensitive skin, and the reddening can be caused either by parasites or by eczema. Once the source of the trouble has been diagnosed and the right treatment found, the complaint disappears in a few weeks, and the hair returns to its original white colour.)

The gait. Kuvasz are large dogs, with sound and strong bone structure, good muscles and corresponding purposeful movement at the walk, and a long ranging trot. Kuvasz are able to trot for 25–30 kms at an even speed without any effort.

Breed Characteristics. The Kuvasz is a well built dog without any coarseness. A strong and vigorous guarding dog, its lean head with straight profile line indicates high physical stability. This trait may also be detected in the lean bone structure and articulation. The slanting eyes are special, quite unlike those found in any related kind. The coat is somewhat coarse, slightly wavy, never fine or silky, which is also a feature unique to this breed. Many of the related breeds have features which are undesirable, and thus considered

50 The Kuvasz as illustrated in 1850
51 An illustration from the beginning of the 19th century shows that while the Puli drives the herd, the Kuvasz guards it
52 A painting from 1855 shows a Kuvasz similar to the present standard

53 Strong, two-year old Kuvasz bitch
54 Small dog in a big kennel
55 A large Kuvasz litter

56 Training of Kuvasz puppies
57 Four-week-old Kuvasz puppy
58 Five-week-old Kuvasz puppy
59 Well-developed, good type Kuvasz bitch
60 Well-developed Kuvasz bitch, with good body
61 Ten-month-old, well-developed Kuvasz puppy with adolescent type coat

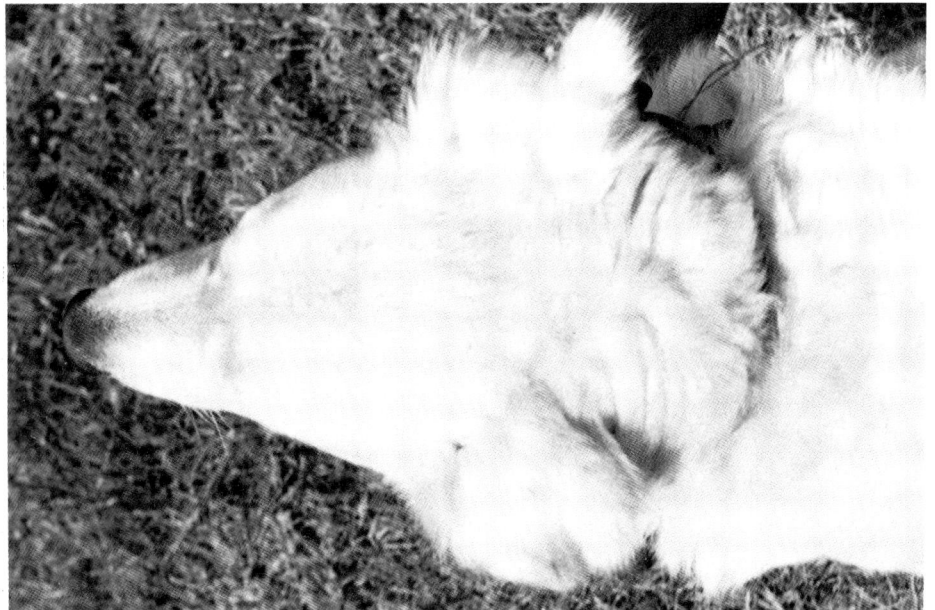

62 The most beautiful part of a Kuvasz's body is its head. The ideal bitch-head
63 A well-built Kuvasz dog's head seen from above
64 Three-month-old Kuvasz bitch puppy
65 Obedience training

66 Kuvasz bitch, ideal coat and set of tail

67 Kuvasz bitch with a beautiful head and fine eyes

68 A strong Kuvasz dog

as faults, such as loose eyelids or lips, heavily pronounced line, a huge or a wide head, shallow cheeks, overpadded joints, straight shoulders, long or smooth hair.

We have enough Kuvasz of pure blood at present to raise the standard of selection very high indeed.

Dogs are easily distinguished from bitches. Dogs are larger in size, more heavily built, with more abundant muscles, bigger bones and larger heads. Even their voice is deeper. Bitches are more delicate and feminine. The head is longer, the structure of the body and limbs is finer. To spoil this difference would be a mistake. Nevertheless dogs should not be allowed to become too coarse and lethargic, and bitches should not be too delicate.

Kuvasz should show the characteristics of their own sex and not those of the opposite. Delicate dogs and rough bitches cannot be good partners in breeding, and their ability to perpetuate good quality characteristics can also be questioned.

Kuvasz were created for fighting and the whole of the body emphasizes this. To endure heavy work the chest had to be deep and well developed, the legs long and well muscled, the teeth strong and long, the neck medium short and rich in muscles. These parts of the body are vitally important for the Kuvasz. A Kuvasz always looks attractive, even when ungroomed and working. The harmonious body structure is enhanced by the texture and colour of the hair.

The destructive effect of undernourishment during World War II can be still felt, since up to the Sixties it was difficult to achieve a uniform size and weight in the whole litter.

Today's puppies reach the desired size and weight easily and develop satisfactorily. The defect in size of the older generation is an unfortunate factor which has to be reckoned with. The standard description has to be strictly applied, even though the majority of our present day stock may not reach it.

Standard height of the Kuvasz's withers, measured with a stick: dogs 71–75 cm, bitches 66–70 cm.

The comparative measurement of the different part of the body given as a percentage of the height of the withers:

	Minimum required according to standard description	often
length of the trunk	104	108–110
depth of the chest	48	52–58
width of the chest	27	–
circumference of the body	120	125–130
length of head	45	–
muzzle in proportion to the length of the head	42	50
length of the ears in proportion to the length of the head	50	–

Weight: dogs 40–52 kgs, bitches 30–42 kgs.

The tables below give information about the ideal development of pups still on the dam, and young weaned puppies.

The average weight of pups still on the dam in grams.

At birth	1	2	3	4	5	6	7
	weeks old						
470	700	940	1,400	1,880	2,780	3,760	4,800

The average weight of puppies after weaning in kgs.

Puppy's sex	3	4	5	6	9	12
	months old					
dogs	12	17	21	25	33	38
bitches	8	12	15	18	23	28

It is essential to create the right environment for the young puppies to develop so that they can meet all the requirements of the standard description. Puppyhood determines the future abilities of all large dogs. Essential food supply is of the highest importance in creating healthy development. Lack of care or the right kind of nourishment will always result in faulty development, and Kuvasz puppies suffering from malnutrition will grow into small adults even though their diet had been corrected at a later stage of their development.

When judging the physical development of a fully grown Kuvasz one must be particularly careful not to attribute malformations of the body that resulted from malnutrition to inherited characteristics.

Condition. Kuvasz are a wiry and well-muscled type of dog, by no means stocky. Lack of exercise and work has very bad effect on a Kuvasz's physical resistance, the shape of the paws and the proportions of the body.

When Kuvasz are kept in a natural environment, and are given plenty of nourishing food, we can be sure of their perfect and healthy development. The condition of the muscles is highly important. Overweight dogs are less likely to be good breeders or parents, breeding of such animals can present a lot of problems.

Temperament. Lively temperament is essential in this breed, since the original work they were meant for demanded quick reactions and the ability to attack. Kuvasz should be kept only in an environment which would still demand similar task. Kuvasz should not be demoted to mere pets, choose some other breed for that purpose.

Lively temperament quickly reflects the impulses and influences of the environment—a favourable environment can create a Kuvasz with a delightful nature while harsh treatment will certainly produce rough and bad tempered dogs.

Kuvasz do not tolerate unjust and undeserved punishment. It is wise not to interfere with their possessions—food and home, or else unpleasant confrontations may arise. Kuvasz do not like the feeling of insecurity and frustration. If a Kuvasz is kept on a chain all the time it is most probable that he will become uncontrollable. Being tied, he cannot defend himself and is open to unjust insults which awake his fury. Once a Kuvasz had been subjected to this sort of a life he will attack all but those few people whose superiority he will be willing to acknowledge. This sort of attitude is, however, most unlikely to arise amongst Kuvasz that are kept in the open and are allowed to roam free.

Kuvasz should never be disturbed while eating. If a bitch is removed from her mate, or if they are disturbed while resting, or are beaten without justification, it is very likely that they will attack.

It is very difficult to tame a Kuvasz which has been subjected to bad treatment. But even in extreme cases, there may be certain people they might respond to. Since unjust beating is handed out by men most of the time, it sometimes happens that the animal will still respond kindly to women.

Puppies of fierce parents prove clearly that rough behaviour is brought about by bad treatment, since given a new and more understanding environment, the puppies will grow into healthy tempered adult dogs.

Ability to learn. Kuvasz were used for guarding duties century after century. The police tried to train Kuvasz for police work and found that their eagerness to attack and their daring was great but they were more difficult to handle and train than German shepherd dogs (Alsatians). Although white proved to be a very useful colour for the shepherd in helping him to tell his Kuvasz from the wolf in a fight, it seemed to be quite a drawback in chasing a criminal. The police abandoned the idea of using Kuvasz as police dogs. In private training, on the other hand, Kuvasz proved to be as highly intelligent as German shepherd dogs, Dobermanns, or Boxers.

There is no need to train a Kuvasz for guarding a house and its grounds, for it will do this by instinct. It forces the intruder to stop, and does not let him move until its master comes.

Soundness of the body. A well developed body consists of strong muscles and bones, lean ligaments, tight skin. Kuvasz were always able to work hard, walk or run for miles, eager to attack and show health and vitality. These qualities must be strictly retained in future breeding. Signs betraying physical slackness cannot be tolerated (drooping eyelids, fleshy lips, etc.). Too light or over-refined physiques are equally undesirable.

Breeding. Breeding Kuvasz faced its most critical period at the time of the Kuvasz's transition from the guarding duties near the herds to living and working in villages and around country houses. The pureness of the breed was in danger. Thanks to the efforts of dog breeders Kuvasz succeeded in overcoming this problem.

When should breeding begin? Young Kuvasz reach sexual maturity at nine months. This is no time, though, to start breeding them. At the age of nine months a Kuvasz bitch has already reached her 26 kgs, which is the ideal weight for a fully grown bitch. The bitch is also mature sexually, but it is wiser to wait until she is about 12–15 months, since the present aim in breeding is to create Kuvasz that will grow bigger than members of past generations. Dogs could also start breeding at this age, only mating two or three bitches to show the dog's ability to pass on the required qualities. Later, when good inheritance is undoubtedly proved, at the age of two, full breeding can begin.

To choose the right sire is very important, especially when certain inherited faults need correcting in the new generation. Dogs that are successful at dog-shows are not always the best quality for breeding. If a dog is highly attractive to look at and also produces excellent puppies he must certainly be considered as a rare example where appearance and temperament are in harmony.

Sires must always be of excellent stock, since one dog can produce 200–250 puppies a year.

The quality of the puppies decides the success of the breeding. Puppies can be judged from the very first days. If the sire and the dam do not live together they should be allowed to play together a few times before the mating. Normally there should be no problem with the bitch. Litters are usually large, on average 9–10 puppies in a litter, but even 12 are common.

Bitches having their first litter should feed a maximum of 6 puppies. More experienced bitches can successfully nurse 8 puppies, although feeding must be supervised. It is advisable to find a foster mother for the rest of the puppies in case there are more in the litter than eight. Pregnant bitches must have a vitamin and protein rich diet. If the bitch is deprived of a nourishing diet the puppies may die soon after birth.

Living conditions. Kuvasz are not very particular about their kennel. Their thick coat gives excellent protection from harsh weather. They only seek the comfort of the kennel in extremely bad weather, but the kennel must always be large and comfortable.

Ideal measurements for a dog house: width 90 cm, length 130 cm, height at the eaves 70 cm, maximum height 100 cm. The door must be at least 40 cm wide and 70 cm in height. The roof must be constructed so that it can be lifted off for cleaning the dog house or attending the puppies. Taking cold weather into consideration, the dog house could be divided into an "antichamber" and sleeping quarters by nailing a piece of board into the dog house, low enough for the Kuvasz to step over. Taking into consideration the prolificacy of the Kuvasz and the quick growth of the puppies, the place of confinement and the young puppies' home must be larger than the ordinary dog house. The width and length must be both increased by 15–20 cm. The threshold must be at least

20 cm high, to prevent the puppies from leaving the dog house before they are three weeks old.

If Kuvasz are kept in a kennel, one must make sure that there is plenty of shade, otherwise in hot weather Kuvasz will suffer a great deal and will lose their appetite. There must always be plenty of fresh drinking water available.

Feeding. There is significant difference in the diet of puppies, fully grown adult dogs and lactating bitches. The adult dog proves to be undemanding in comparison to other, similar type of breeds. On the average a Kuvasz needs 1/4 or 1/3 less food than other dogs of the same weight. Their daily diet normally consists of a mixture of cereal, meat and leftovers from the kitchen. Different dog cereals—supposing these contain animal protein and added vitamins—are also suitable.

Puppies need plenty of food. Well nourished puppies will grow into healthy adult dogs. Up to the age of three weeks milk alone is sufficient, but from then on their diet must be supplemented. Sometimes it is wiser to start mixed feeding at two–two and a half weeks. One can begin by giving the puppies milk that has been previously boiled and then cooled, or milk with cereal. Gradual weaning is important since it eases the bitch's duties and helps the puppies to develop sooner and quicker. If weaning does not take place at this early stage but the bitch is allowed to feed the puppies without any outside help she will become weak and will lose considerable weight.

Absolute weaning will be due at seven weeks. Every puppy should be "greedy" by this age. The first worming of the puppies should be carried out before the total weaning, and the bitch should be wormed at the same time.

After weaning the puppies should be fed at least twice a day, but three feeds a day are even better. The most nourishing food is meat. The shepherds always had a piece for their dogs.

Chewing helps develop teeth. Especially if the puppies are on cereal diet, a bone should always be given to nibble on.

Minerals and vitamins must form an essential part of the puppies' diet. Meat, blood, milk, liver, eggs are all highly rich in vitamins. Kuvasz often need extra vitamins—A and D in particular—especially during wintertime. These can be given either in pills or can be injected. Lack of these vitamins can result in the unsatisfactory development of the bone structure (rickets) which is easier to prevent than to cure.

The perfect condition of the pregnant bitch guarantees the good physical qualities of the puppies. Bitches should not be allowed to become overweight though, since it might be dangerous to the pregnancy itself or the confinement. Fat bitches are less able mothers, and can also easily suffocate their puppies.

Grooming. The coat of a Kuvasz never gets felted and matted. The hair is relatively harsh so dirt and mud easily fall off it. A Kuvasz coat does not need much grooming at all. The only problem there might be is how to keep it white and shining. Kuvasz should only be bathed very rarely, and the coat should preferably be brushed, not combed. Their bed must always be kept clean. The dog house is best lined with straw, hay or bracken. Puppies should also be placed on soft, dry and clean straw or hay as this can easily be changed.

The openings of the body should be wiped clean with a wet sponge. Sticky eyes must also be wiped regularly, especially during puppyhood. Dew claws must be removed.

Judging Kuvasz

The purpose of judging new-born puppies is to sort out the ones that could never develop into adequate breeding material. If the parents are purebred Kuvasz it is highly unlikely that the puppies will be parti-coloured or other colour than white.

When there are more than seven puppies to a litter, and the litter is of good quality, a foster mother must be found. New mothers should not feed more than six puppies, while older bitches can keep eight for feeding.

The degree of pigmentation can be successfully established in the first two weeks after birth. If the skin has grey colouring the puppies will be of good quality. It happens more and more often that the puppies show already at birth grey colouring even on the sole-pads and the belly. The nose will become slate grey by the end of the first week. The colour of the sole-pads can be decided by the third week of life. The most regular development is a gradual darkening of the solepads. The same could be said about the pigmentation of the belly, the colour gradually gets darker, until the whole will become uniformly grey. Serious faults are: parti-coloured (butterfly) nose, eyelids or lips; or flesh colouring of the belly and the sole-pads. Individuals showing these signs should not be used in breeding. Very short, smooth hair is also a serious fault, it will never improve to the requirements of the standard description.

If we observe puppies while playing or during feeding-time we get a good picture of the tail carriage by the time of weaning. It will be obvious which will carry his tail over his back, which will let it droop. The latter carriage is the right one.

Faulty bites can also be detected by this age. A definite opinion can be formed about pigmentation and the position of the ears at about 3 months of age.

The puppy's coat is more woolly than a fully grown dog's, even on those parts of the body which will be later covered with short, straight hair (head, ears and the limbs). Soft hair is natural during the early months, but should stiffen later on. Besides the above mentioned points we should carefully examine the size and physical strength of each puppy.

How to judge the fully grown Kuvasz. Judging should always begin by watching the Kuvasz in motion. When the Kuvasz is moving it is easy to see the proportion and the movement of the limbs, or the different faults of the movement which would influence the whole of the physique or are not in accordance with the breed characteristics. Next comes the partial judging of each section of the body. With the Kuvasz all parts can be seen and easily judged. When judging the different sections of the body the Kuvasz must take an "open standing" position (the legs on the judge's side must be slightly apart, while the ones on the far side closer to each other) but also should be made to move a few steps from time to time, so the setting of the head, the angle of the neck and the tail carriage can also show up.

General impression should be formed when a quick judgement is needed, i.e., to establish the breed characteristics.

To classify the animals at shows in only possible after each member of the breed has been judged.

It is possible to differentiate quality by giving points, since the sections of the body can be so easily seen, but this method takes a long time. It is more expedient to describe each part, deciding whether it is good, or not, whether a fault can pass, or makes the dog altogether unsuitable for breeding.

What work are Kuvasz meant to do? The original duty of the Kuvasz was to guard herds and cattle. Nowadays this purpose cannot be the only reason for work—looking after and protecting homes, buildings, manor houses, factories, building sites, etc. They top the list of all guard dogs because of their courage, loyalty and daring. If a Kuvasz is in charge of a larger territory—an estate or factory—he should always know and belong to one person, for instance a night watchman.

Kuvasz are excellent for guarding homes and gardens. They walk around in the garden and do not tolerate strangers at all. The place one dog is allocated to look after should not be larger than 1–1.5 acres.

It is very important to train a Kuvasz. He responds naturally to the ancient instinct of protecting and guarding without special training. No stranger can escape once within the boundaries of a Kuvasz's territory; he would not let them go or move until he is ordered to do so by his master. But they certainly must be trained for tracking or to perform any other specialized duties. In former centuries Kuvasz were successfully trained and used for hunting, mainly wild boar. Their courage and toughness fitted them well for this task.

Trained Kuvasz look after children carefully, they guard all the children in their master's family, but usually do not trust anybody else. They are not overfriendly, but nevertheless they are often kept nowadays as pets since they are so attractive with their extraordinary white coat and beautifully harmonious built.

The Komondor

(Canis familiaris pastoralis villosus hungaricus. Raitsits, 1924)

Origin. The earliest written record of the word "Komondor" to denote a Hungarian breed of sheep dogs dates from the year 1544. The records of the 1600s give a picture of the Komondor's work as well. Amos Comenius writes in 1673: "Komondoroc oerzic a csordat" (in ancient Hungarian: "Komondors guard the herd"). Another author, Ferenc Pethe, in his *Natural History and Professional Sciences* calls the Komondor the "Leader of the dogs" on account of his singular appearance.

The opinion of the linguists is divided as far as the origin of the word is concerned, but with the help of earliest written records it has been proved that herdsmen used Komondors as guards "from the beginning of time". There are scientists who consider the word to be Turkic-Pecheneg. Others believe it to have originated from either Turkish, Latin, Italian or French.

The first illustration of an early Komondor appears in Ferenc Pethe's *Natural History and Professional Sciences* in 1815 (Fig. III). This picture not only gives information about a Komondor's shape, the different parts of the body but also about his temperament and physique. Another photograph from the beginning of the 1900s shows a Komondor whose perfect appearance could be taken as an example to our present day breeders. Of all the ancient breeds of Hungarian sheep dogs this is the one breed which had a uniform appearance even in the earliest times, and which went through the least changes.

What produced this special breed, under what circumstances and with what purpose in mind? Among the contributing factors were, in addition to the practical breeding efforts of the shepherds, the climatic and geographical features of the Asian and European steppes. The sheep dog that had to guard the flocks had to endure the extremes of the continental climate: the 30–40 °C of summer days just as well as the wind and freezing temperature of 30–40 °C of the winters. It was the Komondor's own coat and not the shepherd's little hut that protected him from the harshness of the climate. The profuse hair provided natural insulation, and also served as protection against wolf bites.

During the period of nomadic shepherding life the wealth of the community was measured by the quantity and quality of the herds and animals in its possession. The herd had to be protected at all cost, against all strangers. There were plenty of predators, both human and animal who cast envious eyes at the sheep and cattle as a source of food. Herds had to be protected day and night. The Komondor took up position near the herd, and no living creature could pass within his boundary. He would face any approaching stranger and attack, leaping onto the intender. The bite of his powerful teeth was deadly or at least bone-breaking.

Komondors have been faithful companions of Hungarian shepherds all through the centuries. In return for their services the shepherds honoured them

XI A strong Kuvasz male

XII Kuvasz bitch with the ideal head
XIII Excellent head of a Kuvasz
XIV Wavy-haired Kuvasz male with well-shaped ears

XV Eight-week-old Komondor puppy with silky baby coat
XVI Six-week-old Komondor puppies
XVII Komondor male, used as guard dog

XVIII Some air at last!
XIX Well-proportioned Komondor male, with good build
XX Well-developed Komondor male

69 Strong, well-developed Komondor bitch

70 Two-year-old Komondor bitch, with a somewhat too fine and open coat

71 Seven-week-old Komondor puppies
72 Komondor bitch with her five-week-old litter
73 Two-month-old Komondor puppies from the same litter
74 Two-and-a-half-month-old Komondor puppy of excellent type
75 A well-coupled Komondor bitch with her four-month-old puppies

76 Well-groomed ribbon-type coat on a huge Komondor dog. International champion

77 Well-proportioned, well-groomed, five-year-old Komondor dog, with a very good head and a fine-ribbon coat

78 A "stripped" old Komondor dog with ideal tail carriage

79 "Stripped" bitch, with a half-grown coat

80 Even from behind the bushy hair, the Komondor sees perfectly

81 Excellent type, four-year-old Komondor male with a corded coat

82 Well-developed nine-month-old Komondor bitch, still in "puppy coat"

83 Well-developed, well-proportioned 18-month-old Komondor bitch. Her coat tends to felt

84 Three-year-old Komondor dog with an ungroomed, felted and matted coat. A well-proportioned head, good constitution

85 Ungroomed, almost matted coat (three-year-old Komondor dog)

86 18-month-old Komondor bitch with a wide-ribbon coat

Drawing of a Komondor from 1815

and only bred the best specimens. Some early record lead us to believe that the heavy thick pelts of the Komondors were sheared in the spring by the shepherds, especially after whelping. Komondors in such state could have easily been taken for a Kuvasz by a non-expert. These two different breeds were very often confused in ancient written records, pictures or in folklore, and it is likely there was crossbreeding of these two separate breeds. The question of how the two breeds became separated is still unanswered. Did they have different roles and duties in the life of the herding community, or were they separated by geographical borders; the fact remains that each breed existed independently of the other.

Changes and Developments of the Komondor in the Course of Time

The only real difference between present day Komondors and the Komondors at the turn of the century is in their size. The increase in size is probably due to richer food and better husbandry. The uniformity of the breed has not changed much in any other way. It is not possible to state when changes took place in the evolution of the breed. Nevertheless we would like to explain a few modern developments. The nomadic way of life required the Komondor to be a valiant guard to the herd. The conformation of the dogs was not so important, as long as they excelled in their work. The 1910–1930s were decisive years as it was then that registered selective breeding started. Significant changes in the use of Komondors took place together with a marked interest shown by professional dog breeders, who aimed at creating an aesthetically more attractive breed. Breeding enthusiasts found it "exceedingly difficult" to tolerate the shaggy coat of the old-fashioned Komondor. Coats that kept cleaner and needed less care were favoured. This is why the "old-fashioned" shaggy, unkempt coat was gradually replaced by more manageable kinds.

Shepherds wanted to keep Komondors white because it helped them to identify the dogs at night but they did not mind pale spots or a yellowish shade. Nowadays white colouring is one of the most important requirements.

The degree of the pigmentation of the skin interested the shepherds only because deeply pigmented skin tends to be tougher than skin with light pigmentation. Today's standard requires dark pigmented skin—especially lips and eyelids—and is an important component of the breed characteristics.

Old pictures show Komondors to be prick-eared, but this feature is due to cropping of the ear which was widely practised in the early days. If the ear's natural shape had been pricked it would most certainly have reappeared again and again in later generations. Photographs that have been left to us, and present day breeding, all prove that Komondors have relatively large and definitely drooping ears. The Komondor does not move its ears even when the dog is in an alert, watchful position.

Related breeds. Sheep dogs resembling Komondors can be found in many countries of Europe and Asia. Their common characteristics are: longer than average coat, a large body, and the work as guard dogs near herds. Many of the breeds went through significant changes as shepherding died out. Some breeds displaying similar characteristics are: in Asia the Kirghiz and Afghan sheep dogs, in Europe the old English (bobtail) and the old German shepherd dogs as well as the Bergamasque, French, Icelandic and Norwegian sheep dogs. The largest dog of this family and the one that has best retained its original and attractive appearance is the Komondor. Today the breed can be found in West Germany, Switzerland, Holland, as well as Canada, the USA, and Great Britain.

Standard Description

Shepherds used Komondors and kept the breed alive up to recent times, although when defending the flocks from wolves was no longer important, there was a great drop in the number of Komondors. A few pairs of dogs were still kept by certain families, and some outstandingly attractive Komondors became pets, or were used for guarding property. Fortunately, this change in use did not result in a deterioration of the dog's good qualities.

The two earliest descriptions of the Hungarian guarding sheep dogs date back to 1767 and 1815. Breed characteristics were first recorded in 1841, and other references followed later.

The first group of organised supporters of Hungarian sheep dogs were those dedicated to breeding Komondors, and in 1924 the Komondor Club was formed. Since then many standard descriptions have been laid down. The best of these was the one by Professor Anghi in 1935. At the beginning of the same year in *The Pedigree Book of Hungarian Dogs* there are 1,700 entries for Kuvasz, 992 for Puli, 293 for Pumi and 972 for Komondors, indicating that after the

Kuvasz, Pulis and Komondors were the most favoured breeds. The standard description used today was set up in 1960, and was acknowledged by the FCI, and is filed under No. 53/b. A detailed study of the breed was completed in 1966.

General Impression. Komondors are associated with dignity in people's mind partly because of their size and partly because of their reserved behaviour. Komondors are not servile, and only young puppies romp and play. The striking thing about a Komondor's appearance is his coat, which is quite unique. As his whole body is covered by masses of long hair, his eyes can hardly be seen. Consequently it is difficult to guess his mood. This masking of his features only strengthens the feeling of respect the Komondor commands. The body is slightly rectangular. The low-set tail gives the impression that the body is longer than it really is. The head looks like a ball of hair rising above the level of the trunk, only the black nose and red tongue being visible. The limbs are straight, strong and well boned and are covered by long hair.

When judging Komondors by general impression at a show, let us remember that these dogs are suspicious and uneasy in a strange environment. In their bearing there is always a mixture of dignity and apprehension. When in unfamiliar surroundings Komondors lack confidence and do not make the best of themselves. They only reveal their true personalities in their usual environment.

The appearance of the dog can be greatly affected by the state of the coat which has many variations. The coat that is considered most attractive can only be found on Komondors of a certain age and even then it does not remain constant. It is easy to misjudge an animal that is brought to a show when immature or at an impropitious moment. Most Komondors, especially bitches used for breeding, are not in full coat during most of their lives. It is important to breed dogs with good coats, although the ideal can generally only be maintained for a short while. It is the character and temperament that is most important when judging this breed. Komondors hardly ever bark during the daytime. They like to retire to a quiet place where they can see and hear everything that is going on and keep a watch on their territory. Their deep and resonant bark is heard only at night but even then only if there is a good reason. They attack boldly, usually jumping on the victim from the front trying to bring him to the ground; in this the Komondor usually succeeds, due to the weight of his body. Once the victim has been brought to the ground, the Komondor does not continue the attack unless provoked. Komondors do not seek friendship but do not tolerate being insulted either.

Description of the Parts of the Body

The Komondor's *head* is in proportion to his large body and although it is richly covered by long hair it should not look coarse or be too large. In plain view the head looks oval, narrowing towards the nose. The widest part of the head measured between the ears, equals the width of the upper jaws, and the length of the muzzle is shorter than the length of the skull. The length of the head is 40–41% of the height at the withers. The muzzle is straight and broad, blunt at the nose. The profile of the head looks circular on well-coated Komondors. Dogs that have just shed their coat show a different shape since the contours can then be seen. The head of the bitch is slightly longer and finer, while males tend to have more rounded heads. The top of the head is well domed and wide, the stop is more pronounced than that of a Kuvasz, but less so than that of the St. Bernard. The nose is very well pigmented and fleshy, the nostrils are wide. The jowls are round, well muscled and the jaws are strong. The lips cover the teeth closely, they are slightly fringed near the corners of the mouth, but no dewlap is permitted. In front view the skull is domed and wide with accentuated brow bones. The eyes are dark brown and almond-shaped, tightly covered by slate grey lids. The eyes should not be visible as the long hair that covers the head makes a natural sunshade. The head is carried at an angle of cca. 40° to the body. The ears are set on the wide, domed skull at medium height, hanging flat and close to the cheeks, the leathers being U or V shaped. The ears are not mobile even in a state of alertness or attack. Cropping of the ears is forbidden.

The neck is carried at an angle of 35° to the horizontal when the dog is alert and observant. In repose the neck is held nearly horizontal.

The neck is of medium length, the male animal having generally a shorter neck than the bitch. There is no ruff of hair or loose skin. Since the head, the neck, the shoulders and the ribs are thickly covered by hair the only way to assess shape and muscular development is by manual examination. (This process might be a little dangerous with strange Komondors.)

Komondors have high and well-developed withers, making the back seem short. The shoulder blades of very young puppies or adults with a weak constitution may be too upright, producing loose elbows.

The withers, the back and the loins are strongly muscled, broad and strong. If these parts of the body lack the necessary amount of muscles or are narrow and lean, the hair parts all along the spine showing even the skin in extreme cases.

A Komondor with a long weak back will never make a strong guard dog. Narrow loins can also be the cause of poor movement.

The croup is wide with an abundance of tough muscles. The tail is set low and must be carried down. The pelvis must be wide—in bitches to assure easy whelping; in dogs width is required to emphasize strength and stability of the whole body.

The top line is straight, with a slight drop towards the tail. This harmonious backline suggests strength and majesty, making the Komondor very impressive.

The rib cage is long and deep, the ribs well sprung, the brisket is wide and well muscled.

The belly should not sag.

The tail is set and carried low, only the tip curves slightly upwards. When the dog is alert the tail may rise to continue the line of the back.

The genitals should be well-developed and both testes should be descended into the scrotum in the adult. Monorchid dogs should be excluded from breeding.

Komondors are usually reserved and discerning in the company they choose. They do not tolerate interference by strangers. Their libido is not high, they prefer to mate with bitches that they know and like. Today breeders want large litters, so strains that breed well and early are favoured.

The front legs are strong, rounded and straight. When Komondors have good coats it is most difficult to judge their shape since they are covered with thick, long hair. The only way to assess their features is by using indirect methods. Weak withers, loose shoulders, elbows that point out are all signs of a slack body, poor rearing and lack of exercise. Puppies can be improved if given plenty of exercise. The points of the shoulder blades should be in line with the brisket. In Komondors with extremely deep chests the elbow may come above the lower line of the chest. If the rib cage is small and inadequate, the elbow joints become visible, and stand away from the body. This is a serious fault, because it means less space for the heart and lungs.

The front legs are straight, the front is not excessively wide. A large brisket with a wider front is not a fault if the limbs are well articulated with the body, but narrow-fronted or "fiddle-fronted" Komondors must be very strictly judged. Komondors are heavily built and the limbs must carry a lot of weight —so lack of support can endanger the whole balance of the body.

It is only possible to get a correct picture of the position of the hind legs in the first nine months of a Komondor's life, later on there is far too much hair on the hindquarters.

The hindlegs should support the trunk at a rather steep angle. But, on the other hand, too steep, strait hindquarters result in a stilted gait, and the shaggy fur tends to hang in ugly narrow lumps on such animals. Weak and narrow hindquarters spoil the whole picture. Both thighs and second thighs must be well-covered in muscle and the stifle well angulated. The hocks should stand approximately under the rump.

The paws. Hair should be trimmed out between the toes before a Komondor is shown, otherwise the paws might appear "soft" because of the long hair that covers them and the ground around them.

Soft or too steep pasterns are equally undesirable. Paws on the front legs can be rounded, on the hindlegs a longer, narrower foot is allowed. Nails must be strong but not too long. Dew claws must be removed.

Skin. The Komondor's skin contains plenty of dark pigment, consequently it is slate-grey, even when the colour of the hair is white. Since the natural colouring of the skin is dark, Komondors are not albinos. Albino spots or features on a Komondor must be treated as a serious fault.

The colour of the hairless parts of the body (the nose, eyelids, lips, pads and nails) must be either black or dark slate-grey. Light coloured nails can be allowed and are not considered to be a serious fault.

It is an advantage if the gums and the palate also have dark colouring. Skin showing in between the hair must be dark.

Lighter spots on the gums and the palate are not a serious disadvantage but light pigment on the nose, the eyelids or on the lips disqualify a Komondor for breeding. Light colouring of the eyes is an equally bad fault. It is one of the most important aims of selective breeding that only Komondors with perfect pigmentation should be used. Occasionally nose pigmentation will fade near the end of winter, or because of whelping or some kind of illness. The nose colour can then vary from light grey even to flesh colour. This symptom should disappear as soon as the cause is eliminated, and it can be prevented by correct diet and keeping the dog in good condition.

Puppies show dark colouring on the hair-free parts of the body at 2–3 weeks old. The pads darken last. After the third week parti-colouring of the nose, eyelids, or the lips cannot be tolerated.

The coat. A Komondor impresses not only by his size and dignified behaviour but by his remarkable coat of hair, the unique feature of the breed. Old documents describe this hair as shaggy, fuzzy, matted or tousled, etc. The structure of the coat is very similar to that of a Puli's but the difference can easily be demonstrated by comparing a lock of hair of a Komondor with one from a white haired Puli. One can establish without doubt which lock of hair comes from which dog.

Komondors' hair is also composed of rough top coat and finer woolly undercoat. The fine coat does not contain medullary substance while the rough upper hair is thicker with medullary substance. The Komondors' top coat and woolly undercoat are thicker and stronger than in Pulis, and the quantity of top coat is slightly greater than it is in a Puli. Old photographs and pictures show the Komondor's hair to be matted, but in a different way to a Puli's matted coat, because of the large body and the slow dignified movement of Komondors. The armour-like mats of hair which are such a serious fault with Pulis can not be seen on Komondors. The best known formations are the following: *matted hair, wide ribbons, tassels, ribbons* and even plain *corded* ones. This last formation deserves a little extra consideration. Some experts have already formed suspicions that this characteristic was introduced by cross-breeding with Pulis. The earliest documents on Komondors certainly do not mention corded coats of hair. It is interesting, though, that in both breeds, entirely independent of each other, corded formations can be found. The cords of a Komondor's hair are naturally somewhat thicker, coarser and longer. It can safely be said that the corded formation is a genetically fixed and inheritable feature of which breeders have taken notice only in the last 30 to 40 years but which quickly became popular since.

Komondors without adequate grooming become completely tangled and felted in uneven—sometimes quite large—mats and plates. These wide and flat lumps are worst on the hindquarters and on the thighs. On the rest of the body the mats are smaller and shaggier, due to partial coat shedding. To get rid of this formation on a Komondor presents a more difficult problem than it does with Pulis, as in most cases it is not possible to use the same grooming method.

The more wool Komondors' coat contains, the easier it gets matted.

The wide ribbon form is an attractive formation if it covers the whole body evenly. This form can be considered as a groomed version.

The smaller ribbon form is most pleasing. The whole body, from neck to tail, from the upper line of the trunk down to the paws, is evenly covered in this heavy coat of tassels. This formation suits the Komondor's large body and temperament, but if neglected, it can easily felt into wide ribbons or mats.

Corded coat. The Komondor's hair is thicker and rougher than that of the Puli so, of course, his cords are thicker and longer. Fewer Komondors than Pulis show this coat formation, which, although most attractive, does not really harmonize with the Komondor's robust build, making him look less substantial. This type of coat needs far more grooming than its equivalent in Pulis.

Whelping or lactating bitches shed their coats on the head, the neck, the chest and the front legs. This process could be described as "stripping". This hair loss will also occur when a dog's diet is not adequate either in quantity or in quality. Lack of vitamin A is a known cause of shedding in both male and female. "Stripping" is not a basic fault, only a disadvantage in appearance. One should not take the dogs to a show during this time. Due to the size of a Komondor it may sometimes take up to two years to regrow a full coat. This disadvantage should not lessen the value of an otherwise excellent animal. Some individuals or families do not have shedding problems at all, but others take quite a long time to be in full coat again. Non-shedders are naturally favoured for breeding. In most cases only the hair on the front half of the animals is shed off and on the hindquarters it only gets shaggy, torn and uneven. Shepherds used to say that "the animal has a 'skirt'".

When a Komondor is judged while or after shedding, it is important to know what sort of hair he really has, what his coat would look like in its natural form, and to decide its qualification based on these facts. The fully grown and well-coated Komondor's body should have no short, smooth or stiff hair. The only difference between hair growing on different parts of the body should be in the actual length of the hair. According to Raitsits, these measurements are as follows: around the lips 9 cm, on the cheeks 14 cm, over the eyes and on the crown of the head 16–18 cm, on the ears 13–17 cm, on the neck 10–14 cm, on the shoulders 15–20 cm, on the lower half of the font- and hindlegs 10–13 cm, along the spine 12–16 cm, on the chest and the belly 22–24 cm, on the thighs 20–24 cm, and on the tail 23–27 cm. The hair of new-born puppies is very fine, wavy or nearly straight, and covers the body evenly.

While the puppy is on the dam his hair is fluffy, very fine and shiny. At weaning this type of hair will be replaced by a soft puppy hair, which does not mat.

Puppies between the age of 6–9 months have a teddy-bear like coat. This juvenile coat is longer and more attractive than the same formation on a Puli puppy. This is the age when young Komondors look their best. This is the time to have a thorough look at all the parts of the body because later on the hair will get much longer and judging the animal's real shape and proportions will be more difficult. The amount of wool in the coat will steadily increase and as most of the dead wool does not fall out of the coat, it starts to cause matting.

Komondors with an open, short or even straight coat should not be used in breeding since these formations are alien to breed-characteristics.

Grooming technique is similar to that for the Puli. There are a few points, though, we would like to emphasize: Komondors are one-man dogs, and do not take kindly to handling by strangers. Naturally, this characteristic can be altered by training, but basically every Komondor reacts in the same way. He may tolerate his master grooming his coat, but would most certainly resist a strange hand. Since he does not betray the degree of his indignation by barking or other noise, but attacks immediately, it is wise to be very wary when grooming his coat.

The two formations that need the least care are the smaller and the larger ribbons so these two shapes should be encouraged.

Komondors that have genetically corded hair do not need any special grooming to maintain their shape, but it is not advisable to try and create a corded coat out of hair which is not naturally corded.

Colour of hair. The Komondor's hair colour is white. Old documents and even descriptions from the 19th century mention different colours, e.g. white, grey, yellowish-white, fawn or reddish. Foreign documents talk about parti-coloured or even black Komondors but these must be the result of cross-breeding. Today's standard requirement is white. Komondors are so well-bred nowadays that serious colour faults can rarely, if ever, be found but a really pure white can still present a problem and can only be achieved by frequent grooming and regular bathing.

Komondors that are not bathed often have off-white hair. One variation of this off-white has a yellowish tint. This colour has given rise to much discussion. Some breeders believe that in certain geographical areas and under certain housing systems the otherwise white hair turns yellowish. Others say that experiments had proved that not all originally yellowish-white Komondors lost the yellowish tint when placed in a different environment. This seems to indicate that this yellowish-white colour may be an inherited characteristic, in which case it should be eliminated. New-born puppies and those still on the dam are snow-white, adolescents are also whiter than their fully grown relations.

Movement. Despite his large body and the enormous amount of hair the

Komondor's movement is not clumsy. Komondors move lightly, comfortably but cautiously when on the lead. During the day he does not usually move much, and only leaves his kennel in extreme necessity. In the evening and at night, his movement becomes livelier, his excursions longer. Night watch duties are his favourites, that is the time when he really enjoys moving about.

Komondor puppies are very lively and playful. They start to be more cautious at about six months.

Valued qualities. Komondors are certainly not household pets, by reason of their size if nothing else. Their main purpose is in outdoor guarding duties. Although occasionally Komondors can be found in flats with balconies, kept entirely as pets, their real need is plenty of space or at least a large garden. Their characteristics can best be enjoyed in a suitable environment.

Breed characteristics. This is the most in-bred of all the sheep dogs and consequently shows great homogeneity. Though the breed is one of the most ancient, the typical appearance and the special abilities are obviously results of a careful, consistent breeding. The main breed characteristics can be found in every member of the breed, and they are definitely passed on to the new generations. Komondors can easily be distinguished from any other breed. Their size, the low carriage of the head, the drooping tail, the very shaggy or corded long white hair, the sunshade of hair over the eyes and the shape of the head are all unique to the breed.

Attractive appearance is one of the basic breed characteristics in the Komondors, but the inner qualities, such as their total devotion to their master, their unbribable sense of duty, their unlimited courage and their strength can by no means be ignored. These qualities ensure the Komondor's future not only for specialist hobby breeding but also for a definite practical use.

Sexual characteristics. It is difficult for a non-expert to tell a Komondor's sex by looking at the animal. Experts, on the other hand, well know that despite the thick coat of hair the secondary sexual characteristics of bitches and dogs can be definitely established. It is a useful aim of selective breeding to try and emphasize the difference of the secondary sexual characteristics. Only large males with strong bone structure and well-developed muscles should be used for breeding. Males should excel themselves for courage and readiness to fight. Bitches should be more "feminine", smaller, with a finer bone structure and altogether more refined than the males. This requirement does not mean that bitches should become too delicate, but that dogs ought to be more robust.

The larger size of the males involves a larger and wider head that is also shorter, a more muscular neck, more pronounced withers and a generally wider frame of the body.

Proportions. The harmony of the different parts of the body of a well-coated Komondor is very pleasing. Komondors that just shed their coat may look out of proportions but the lack of a full coat can only be a drawback at shows, and certainly should not influence the decision when judging the animal's potential for breeding. If one does not make every effort to avoid being influenced by a partly shed coat, breeding might suffer in the long run, since a negative decision might be reached.

The thick coat should not serve as a disguise to cover ugly proportions. Serious faults of construction must be discovered and judged severely even if the coat is attractive.

Even though a Komondor's head is covered by long hair it is in reality not too large or heavy, but in proportion to the size of the body. The limbs, which are also thickly covered with hair, are well-built, lean but not heavy or coarse, resulting in a springy but not too light gait.

Development. The Komondor is the largest Hungarian sheep dog. Its height has somewhat diminished because of hardships during World War II and the fact that his original purpose has almost entirely disappeared. The aim of selective breeding to preserve the original size is very important and justified, since a large body is one of the main requirements of guarding watch dogs.

The height of the withers measured by a stick as required by the standard description:

dogs: about 80 cm, but at least 65 cm

bitches: about 70 cm, but at least 55 cm

The comparative measurements of the different parts of the body given as a percentage of the height of the withers:

	at least as in the standard description	often
Length of the trunk	104	100–108
Depth of the chest	45	50–56
Largest point of the brisket	28	30
Circumference of the body	116	120
Length of the head	41	–
Length of the muzzle in proportion to the length of the head	42	–
Length of the ears in proportion to the length of the head	60	–

Weight: dogs 50–60 kg, bitches 40–50 kg.

Weight gain of well developed Komondor puppies:

The average weight of puppies while still on the dam in grams

At birth at	1	2	3	4	5	6	7	8
	weeks							
500	750	1,000	1,500	2,000	3,000	4,000	6,000	8,000

The average weight of puppies after weaning, in kgs.

The puppy's sex at	3	4	5	6	9	12
	months					
dogs	14	23	30	36	41	45
bitches	10	18	25	30	33	35

This process of development can only come about if maximum help is given to the mother to increase the quality of her milk while she is feeding the puppies, and if the puppies receive sufficient supplementary food as soon as they are ready for weaning. This is the only way to achieve the ideal large size.

Condition. The body is richly covered with muscles, and the bone structure is solid. Attention must be given to a well balanced diet from a very early age to help the formation of muscle and bone. Limbs should be wiry, even though abundantly supplied by muscles.

It is impossible for a growing puppy to be overweight. Later in life, once the animal is fully grown, it might put on excess weight through lack of exercise and free movement but this is most undesirable.

Temperament. Seeing a Komondor stretched out under a shady tree in hot summer one would not suspect how ready they are to attack the unwanted visitor. But he always keeps sharp eye on the world around him, and is always on guard. They look secretive because their facial expression cannot be seen, so there is no way of telling their mood. One can only be sure once they start moving. Then their intentions become obvious. Most of the time, this sudden movement means definite action, too. Normally they seem to be cool and calm, rather phlegmatic, but if they decide on action they attack immediately. Komondors rest quietly like Bulldogs, and attack as readily as Schnauzers.

Komondors can be disciplined but should never be punished without good reason. Komondors that had been punished unjustly can become uncontrollable because of unpleasant memories. Being kept on a chain, or tied up can also result in savage behaviour. Komondors that are ill-treated do not pass on bad temperament to the new generation.

Komondors do not try to please and resent being fussed, stroked and treated like pets. Since it is not possible to tell their mood, strangers should always approach them with extreme caution.

Soundness of the body. Sheep dogs that were used for rounding up the cattle on the Puszta were expected to work together with the shepherds. Guard dogs started their duties when the shepherds finished. Komondors guarded the herds at night and in bad weather. They had to put up with all the extremes of the weather on the Puszta. Their large body, phlegmatic and at the same time fiery temperament was coupled with a very sound constitution. Komondors unable to withstand the hardships of the life on the Puszta, those with slack bodies, or no eagerness to fight did not survive.

Ability to learn. One might think that there never was a real need for Komondors to be intelligent animals, since what was required of them came naturally and the desire to live and survive fights was inborn, but surprisingly, Komondors are highly intelligent, and eager to learn. Some Komondors are known to be the "guards" of manor houses and farms, others have been used as gun-dogs because of their excellent sense of smell. Some were trained by the police both in Hungary and in Germany, with very good results. Most of all they are extremely talented guard dogs, protecting cattle from wolves, and, if necessary, one human being from another.

Readiness to fight, a good nose and a high intelligence are all breed-characteristics, but sometimes Komondors can be very stubborn. But when they are obstinate, harsh punishment only makes them sullen.

Type and constitution. Komondors are large guard dogs, still retaining their original abilities despite domestication. The size of the body, the type of bone structure, the temperament, the movement all help the Komondor in carrying out its duties. Komondors should always be given the opportunity of fulfilling their natural task instead of being forced into circumstances which are alien to the breed.

Breeding of Komondors. Breeding is a manifold problem. It is still difficult to find right mating partners, as a sufficient number of high standard Komondors has only recently been reached. About 350 puppies a year are bred which approximately covers the demand. Not so long ago every Komondor was allowed to breed because of the scarcity of the breed after World War II. Today their number is steadily rising, so selective breeding has been started again. As practically every ancestor of the present stock is known to the breeders the hereditary traits of the different couples can be easily calculated. Komondors that are too timid or too delicately built or do not meet the standard requirements are no longer allowed to breed.

Preparation for breeding. The speed of growth and maturity of Komondors is average in animals still kept on the Puszta. Most well nourished puppies in specialist breeder's hands reach their full size by the end of the first year of their life.

In the 1930s it was said that a Komondor should be fully matured by the age of 2, but present day breeding, in aiming to achieve a larger bodily size, has also speeded up the process of maturity. When properly fed, Komondors reach their fully grown size and maximum weight earlier. Young Komondors can be used for breeding as soon as they have reached three-fourth of their full size, which means that breeding starts earlier than when Komondors were kept in the Puszta.

Most bitches come in heat for the first time when they are 9–12 months old, but if a puppy does not develop satisfactorily, this might not be until 6–8 months later. Young bitches should not be allowed to mate at their first heat since they are not yet mature. 50 years ago it was held that growth was only completed after the third year but today bitches can be safely used for breeding once they are 16–18 months old. They can carry and feed 6 puppies without endangering their own health if properly fed.

All good standard puppies should be well looked after, since the number of Komondors is still not high enough. One bitch should not feed more than 8 puppies at a time, so foster mothers must be found.

Dogs can be used at stud once they have reached sixteen months. It is difficult to achieve two litters a year when breeding Komondors. In most cases bitches bear one litter a year. The puppies are born at the end of the winter or the beginning of spring.

Komondors tend to be monogamous and it happens, that dogs that are used to living in pairs are not willing to serve any other bitch than their original partner. An owner had a Komondor dog and an Alsatian bitch. The Komondor was only interested in German sheep dogs and was never willing to mate a Komondor bitch. Komondors are generally faithful to their partner in every way. Unfortunately not all dogs are keen studs and some bitches have a low conception rate. Selective breeding should favour families that breed easily.

Bitches in heat should be taken to the dogs and not the other way round. The prospective partners should be given plenty of opportunity to get to know each other.

There are already some families that excel themselves in transmitting certain characteristics. Line breeding has already been put to practice. Breeders are trying to fix these excellent qualities into well established lines. To avoid the appearance of unwanted features breeders often turn to in-breeding and sometimes to the mating of close relatives. Selective breeding must consider along with the appearance of each Komondor the inner qualities, the level of resistance and a sound constitution.

Living conditions. Komondors that are kept tied to a chain all their lives are certain to become fierce. It is possibly acceptable that the dog should be tied to a chain during the day but he must be set free at night. The best situation is, of course, if he is allowed freedom in the garden and around the house all the time. His usual resting place, or his kennel, should not be approached by strangers. It is best to put up a notice warning people of the presence of a guard dog. Komondors are really hardy and have no special requirements about their dwelling place. They need a resting place in the shade during summer and a corner which would give them shelter from the wind. Generally they only seek a roof against heavy rains. Many of them hardly ever enter a kennel, not even to sleep. The size of the kennel is the same as the Kuvasz's, only the entrance should be slightly taller and wider.

The ideal resting place ought to be somewhere in the yard so that the Komondor can have a clear view of the whole territory he has to protect. Where two Komondors are kept both animals should be provided with separate resting places. When Komondors are kept in kennels there must be enough space for them to move about and they should have sufficient fresh air and shade in hot summer. If they have to be kept in smaller enclosures during the day, they should be allowed to move freely at night. A large open space is needed for keeping this breed.

Feeding. Komondor puppies develop even faster than Kuvasz puppies. At two and a half weeks puppies are ready for solid food. Supplementary milk and cereals given to puppies not only makes the mother's life easier but also produces quicker growth in the puppies.

By the time the puppies are weaned they should be well used to solid food. This means that being deprived of the most nourishing food—their mother's milk—does not result in loss of weight.

When looking after Komondor puppies, worming is most important. If there are a large number of worms in the stomach or in the bowels at weaning time, it is most likely there will be signs of an underdeveloped body, and the general level of disease resistance will be low.

Fully grown Komondors are not choosy about their food. Once they have passed the puppy stage their diet can become much simpler. Offal or meat trimmings can be supplemented by unrefined cereals. Dog meal with meat makes an excellent diet. This, of course, does not apply to puppies who, after weaning, need meat and food that needs chewing to help the teeth and the muscles of the jaw to develop.

Grooming. Puppies must be kept clean by brushing and combing. Once they are five months old the hair should not be combed any more and brushing must also become less frequent. This is the age when the fur starts to develop its later structure. The locks should no longer be brushed thoroughly. On the contrary, formation of even ribbons or cords should be helped by hand and only the matting of larger lumps must be restrained.

Once the adult coat has fully developed the brush can be used again for removing dirt, but without changing the shape of the coat. Changing the shape of the coat of a neglected adult takes time. The flat mats will have to be cut up into strips and worked through by hand to help the felting. Corded hair should only be formed of hair which is genetically corded. To attempt to alter other type of hair into a corded formation means a great amount of extra work, and only causes unnecessary discomfort to the dog.

The eyes must always be kept free of any kind of discharge. Conjunctivitis can be caused by the long hair getting into the eye. The result is a constant unpleasant inflammation, which can only stop once the guilty hair has been removed.

Extra cleanliness is required around the anus and the testicles, and matting must be avoided in these places.

Bitches and dogs must both be prepared for the mating act. Tails and obstructing hair should be tied to one side. Excessive and long hair should be removed from the belly and vulval area of a bitch before whelping to save soiling and to help the new-born puppies to feed. Dew claws should be removed.

Judging Komondors

Since the breed is highly in-bred, the litter should be uniformly white. If other colours or parti-colouring appears the whole litter's pedigree is suspect.

An obvious undershot mouth can be seen at birth. Pigmentation of the skin can be judged when the puppy is three weeks old. If by then the nose, the eyelids and the lips are still flesh coloured they will not improve much with time. Short and smooth hair will not give a perfect adult formation either.

Between three weeks and six months let us not attempt to judge puppies, since they do not show their adult characteristics. They should be given plenty of nourishing food to aid perfect growth.

9–12 months old puppies already show their fully grown proportions. Only the coating is still puppy hair and that will stay until they are two years old. The different parts of the body and the proportions of a young dog about nine months old can be judged since the body is not yet covered by long hair. A correct opinion can also be formed about his carriage and gait. The signs of weakness—a sunken or roached back, soft loins, loose shoulders, elbows and joints, soft paws, and spread toes—must all be judged strictly. If a young dog having plenty of exercise shows a weak structure these faults will become only more acute since as a breed Komondors are not very active when grown up. By this age one can also make good estimate of the final size of the body. By nine months the Komondor arrives at 95–98 per cent of his full size. If a dog lacks height at this age it will never reach the ideal size. Komondors not reaching the height required in the standard description are more like Pulis, and should not be used for breeding.

Komondors that prove to be phlegmatic should also be excluded, but this is very unusual.

The coat should be judged only after the dog is two years old. Komondors with straight, short or loose hair that will not mat or cord cannot be used for breeding.

Komondors must be conditioned for being taken to shows. Since their normal duty is to keep strangers away they are not used to crowds of people; they often resent the multitude of spectators and judges, and try to hide away in a quiet corner. It is nearly impossible to judge such a Komondor because they never show their real qualities. By careful training even a Komondor can be made to behave and obey. They can get used to being led among people and being examined by the judges.

The working behaviour of a Komondor is quite unique. He hardly ever makes a noise, even when he barks it is to draw attention to danger or to frighten an intruder away. Komondors rely entirely on themselves when they are protecting either human beings or property. They stay out of sight until they see the need to attack—making perhaps only a low growl. They jump on the enemy bringing him to the ground by force of the impact. Once the intruder is down they do not harm him, only stand over and restrain him.

There is a great difference between the working methods of the Kuvasz and the Komondor. A Kuvasz would patrol steadily around the territory he is protecting. Komondors hardly ever move, especially during the day or in summer, but they always keep an eye on their kingdom, ready to go into action at any time.

Their method of attack and their bite is dangerous. Many Komondors are used for protecting homes nowadays, where they carry out their duties to perfection. The capabilities of this breed should be put to a still more effective use by training Komondors as guards for large buildings, county estates and factories. They would not let anyone, other than the people they are accustomed to come within reach of the place. They are absolutely trustworthy and cannot be bribed. Komondors are suspicious of strangers and will only accept food from their masters. Komondors are very good as personal bodyguards, and are often used for protecting children, especially abroad.

III. HUNGARIAN HUNTING DOGS

When speaking about hunting dogs, we have to keep in mind that, independent from the actual objective of use, most dogs are suitable for hunting, so the majority can be regarded as hunting dogs. This ancient instinct of dogs was perhaps influenced, weakened or even oppressed through domestication but was not killed completely. Independently from man, dog left to its own devices will still manage to acquire prey and not die of hunger, even if kept in an apartment previously.

Within a breed the methods of hunting developed according to the game that lived at the place of origin. Vizslas, with their excellent nose, were to hunt in bushy, thick ground where game was not visible. The Hungarian Greyhound comes from a territory where swift running game was found. It is able to catch up with a running antelope. In the same way an ancient, inherited instinct with dogs is that while they are indifferent to one kind of game they will follow another passionately. Such interest is manifested by Vizslas for game birds; Greyhounds are predisposed to run after hares while, at the same time, pheasants fail to excite them.

The native Hungarian hunting dog breeds can be divided into three groups:
(1) Vizslas: all-round searching, pointing and retrieving gun dogs;
(2) Hungarian Greyhounds: swift-running dogs; and
(3) Transylvanian Hounds for the hunt.

The Hungarian Vizsla

The Vizsla, especially the short coated variety, is an indigenous Hungarian breed. The origin may have been an eastern hound that came with the Hungarians from Asia, and was then crossed with hounds breed in the country. Very little written material is known about the early development and formation of the breed.

According to G. Wenzel, the Vizsla was known in Hungary already in the reign of the kings of the House of Árpád (11th–14th centuries), but ancient authors give no information regarding them. The fact that the breed had been used in olden times to flush game and when hunting with a net was proved by a letter from 1510 where a man asks his brother for a Vizsla suitable to net quails. The document also tells us why: "Because the Vizsla is a produce of recent times and even here is not only used to point the game but is required to fulfill manifold hunting capabilities and is in possession of such features."

This is all the more possible as formerly most dogs had to be trained to point game.

Diezel-Mika,* in his book *Hunting Dogs,* tells us that the very first individuals of hunting dogs used as Vizslas indicated the characteristics of the basic breed, in contrast to other breeds (though we have no knowledge as to how certain features, e.g. the ears, evolved to their present shape). From this basic type, different types of Vizslas evolved in different regions which were always held in higher esteem by their owners than all other types. The fusion of types was mainly hindered by the difficulty in communication which makes it understandable that even in the middle of our century Vizsla types indicating the original characteristics of hounds were to be seen, regarded as the only possible type by their owners.

The development of the present form of gun dogs (pointers) was begun in the middle of the 19th century. An obvious sign of systematic cynological breeding work was that in 1879, at the Hannover International Dog Show, the experts officially determined the characteristics of pointers. Though these related to German pointers, they were of impact also on the systematic breeding of Hungarian pointers, i.e. Vizslas. According to certain records Poodles also had a role in the development of pointers. These gun dogs went by the name of Russian or Polish water dogs and were used mainly to flush game. According to a record: "The Poodle, if trained, points partridge and hare from quite far, though not as well as pointers, still they can be used successfully in front of a gun."

As is to be seen, the development of the Hungarian Vizsla is the result of systematic cross-breeding. Documents tell us that in the 15th–16th century, scent hounds were used in the then fashionable type of hunting: falconry. During the Turkish occupation of Hungary these dogs were crossed with the yellow hunting dogs of the Turks (16th–17th century). The breed, approximately in its present form, existed already in the 18th century and then, in the course of the 19th century, to improve its good properties, it was cross-bred with English pointers, German short-haired pointers and also blood hounds. The century-long selective breeding finally resulted in the present-day Vizsla. It seems certain that it inherited its capability to point game from the indigenous Pannonian hounds and its colour from the yellow Turkish quail-hunting dog. The wire haired variety has been known about 40 years; here a role was played in its breeding by the German wire-haired pointer.

* Diezel-Mika: *A vadászebek* (Hunting Dogs). Athenaeum, Budapest, no date of publication.

Vizslas are not only highly valued as gun dogs but also because of their beauty, clean coats, and pleasant temperament they are good dogs to have in the house. They are grateful, loyal animals that heap affection on their master and bring joy to their surroundings. They are also very easy to train and thus both huntsmen and people who are fond of hounds are more and more interested in the breed. Nowadays they are known in most European countries and are bred in such a great number in the United States that the American Vizsla Club is operating as an independent organisation within the framework of the AKC (American Kennel Club).

The Hungarian Greyhound (Agár)

Necessity makes a hunting dog of any dog, especially if it is forced to procure its food. In the beginning dogs are said to have followed man and given him some help in bringing down game and so in exchange they received what was left of the meal. However, as man recognized the game-acquiring capabilities of the dog, he tried to utilise them for his own purposes. It is quite possible that even before constructing the bow and the arrow, man was accompanied by dogs more swift than game which helped him to round up the necessary quarry. This could well have been the ancestor of the Greyhound.

The above supposition is made probable by the logical grouping of hypotheses regarding the origin of Greyhounds and, therefore, there are experts who think the origin of these dogs may well have been in certain parts of Africa the home of swift-running game. According to them the type of Greyhound used for its swiftness was developed through selection for fitness. There are also people who believe that its place of origin was Asia. Whatever it may have been, the oldest relics of civilisation, the remnants of the Babylonian and Egyptian culture, wall paintings, the decorations of the Pharaohs' graves and other illustrations all prove that Greyhound-type dogs existed in the very oldest times.

There are no authentic historic documents regarding the origin of the Hungarian Greyhound. It can, however, be supposed that the Hungarian nomadic herdsmen arriving during the migrations from Asia to Europe already had a greyhound-type dog, used to catch running deer. It is quite possible, therefore, that the ancient variety of the Hungarian greyhound got in this way to the Carpathian Basin. Later on, the Turks brought similar dogs from Asia Minor, which interbred with the ones in Hungary and in this way developed the ancestor of the Hungarian greyhound. As they were not only excellent runners but also courageous strong dogs of great stamina, they were not only used for running down hare, but also roe deer, red deer and even wolves. The greyhounds were accompanied by the hunters on horseback—partly to help their hounds if necessary, and also prevent them from tearing the game to pieces.

The Greyhound-type dogs, also the Hungarian Greyhound, the Agár, were the favourites of the nobility in the Middle Ages, not only for their elegance, but also because of their usefulness and because hunting with greyhounds was the fashion of those days.

Parallel to the development of agriculture, areas for hunting with Greyhounds on horseback became more and more restricted. In the second half of the 19th century, when real, scientific breeding started to be established in Hungary, game husbandry was developed and coursing with greyhounds was restricted. At the same time, however, the competitive spirit resulting from breeding also brought about the need for swifter Greyhounds. These were the times when both horses and Greyhounds were imported from Great Britain in large numbers. The breed-transforming crossing with these English Greyhounds resulted in the Hungarian greyhound type of the first half of the 19th century. Restauration of the original type has but recently started.

Instead of actual hunting, Greyhounds are to be seen more and more on racetracks and coursing rounds. This enables a comparison of the animals against each other resulting in a selection based on speed and skill. A number of Greyhound Associations were formed in the last century, coursing competitions developed, in the beginning after live hares in the open fields, later artificial coursings and amateur track races were organized.

The Transylvanian Hound

The conquering Hungarians not only brought hounds with them but probably also found some in the Carpathian Basin, as hunting on horseback was already fashionable at that time. There are no historic documents to indicate as to whether the hounds found by the Hungarians when entering the Carpathian Basin were indigenous or whether they were the legacy of the Huns and Avars passing through before the Hungarians. Dog-bones found during excavations permit to conclude that certain beagle types came to the Carpathian Basin in the times of the Great Migrations.

The Pannonian Hound developed most probably in the Middle Ages when hunting was fashionable all over Europe and the Hungarian packs were certainly cross-bred with foreign hounds. The breed known for a long time as the Hungarian Hound was a result of crossing the Pannonian Hound with the Austrian Bracke and the Polish Ogar Hound. They gained ground mostly in Transylvania, adapted to the environment and the hunting conditions and prevailed there as hunting dogs. Especially the black Hungarian "Beagle" was held in high esteem because of its excellent nose and fearlessness.

Towards the end of the 19th century this Transylvanian Hound was bred in relatively large number and in pure blood all over Hungary. However, by the beginning of the 20th century, as mentioned in a contemporary report, their number diminished greatly and their quality became unsatisfactory. As Diezel-Mika says in his book *Hunting Dogs:* "There are no more Hounds for which anybody would give in exchange a 3-year old Transylvanian colt, as it did happen in former days."

Reconstruction and saving of this interesting, ancient Hound breed should be the aim of present-day Hungarian dog breeding.

The Standard of the Short-haired Hungarian Vizsla

Name: Short-haired Hungarian Vizsla, FCI standard No. 57/c, 1982

General Features, Use

Medium-size, elegantly built, yellow, short-haired hunting dog. Rather light bone structure reflecting harmonious beauty and strength. Well-balanced, intelligent, lively temperament. According to historians, may have the Pannonian Kopó (Hound) as one of its ancestor. The yellow hunting dog the Turks bred certainly played a major role in helping to develop the race.

Certain specialists, however, are of the opinion that the appearance of the Vizsla goes back many centuries. New research indicates the "sloughi" is also an ancestor of the Vizsla. The first specimens of today's breed appeared at the beginning of the 18th century. In accord with modern hunting procedures, several other hunting dog breeds were employed toward its improvement in the 19th century. The result was a yellow-coloured, independent breed of Hungarian hunting dog with a stock which weathered major losses during the Second World War. The modern type is characterized by the following:

The Vizsla can be trained well and easily. It does not withstand harsh treatment well. The Vizsla's good hereditary properties, excellent memory and good combinative capacity make it a first-rate modern hunting dog.

Though passionately fond of hunting, it takes well to being kept in an apartment. This reason, together with its distinguished behaviour, make it a popular pet.

Widely recognized for its excellent acclimatization capability, it is ready to work untiringly, even in very warm weather.

The following hereditary properties must be regarded as fundamental requirements: excellent nose, stable and figurative pointing, distinct trailing and retrieving qualities, love of working in water and excellent response to handling.

The head: dry, noble, well-proportioned. The skull moderately wide, slightly domed. A slight median line divides the top of the head from the moderately developed occipital bone towards the forehead. The stop is always moderate and the bridge of the nose is always straight. The foreface is well-arched, never pointed or wide, ending in a well-developed nose with nostrils well open. When measuring the straight line linking the tip of the nose and the inner corners of the eyes, the foreface should always be considered less than 50 per cent of the total length of the head. The fang is proportionately long. The jaw is well-developed, well-muscled. The teeth are slightly oval. The eyelids are tight. The colour of the eyes matches the coat, and the darker the colour, the more desirable. The ears are of medium length, set back slightly at medium height lying flat against the cheeks. They cover the ear-holes well and end in a V-shape slightly rounded at the tips.

The neck: medium length, well-muscled, slightly arched. Free from disturbing dewlaps. Set on the trunk at medium height.

The trunk: Powerful and well-proportioned, somewhat longer than it appears in quadratic breeds. The withers are pronounced and well-muscled. The back is short and straight, with a tight loin and the upper line slightly rounded at the base of the rump. The chest is moderately wide and extends deeply to the elbows.

The ribs are moderately arched. The shoulders are well-muscled, with blades slanting and capable of moving freely.

The limbs: The forelegs are straight, strong-boned, with elbows close to the body. The hindlegs are well-muscled, moderately angled; hocks are somewhat low-set. The toes are strong, well-rounded, compact, and close to each other, with paws slightly oval. The nails are strong, the pads tough.

The tail: slightly low-set, medium thick, narrowing towards the tip. Three-quarters of the original tail are usually left to form an aesthetic whole, one-quarter is often docked. However, if the fine-lined tail is carried the standard way, i.e. close to the horizontal, docking is not mandatory.

The skin: taut, no wrinkles or folds. Pigmented, the nose flesh-coloured, lips, eye-lids and nails are brown. Pads are slate-grey.

The coat: lies tightly; short, straight, rough to the touch. The belly is covered with light hairs. The hair becomes shorter and more silky at the ears. The tail is covered with longer hair.

The colour: Sand or dark sand-coloured in various shades. Small white spots on the chest and on the end of feet or white hairs are not defaulted.

The gait: far-reaching, vigorous, light. Paces at a balanced steady canter when at work.

The height: The ideal height (measured with a stick) for
males: 56–61 cm
bitches: 52–57 cm

A 4 cm deviation from the above is permitted either way if it does not disturb the harmony. Static and dynamic balance and symmetry are more important than proportions measured in centimetres.

The type-flaws, defects: Structural flaws include anything that adversely affects harmonious movement and ability to work continuously.

Major flaws are an extremely light or rough structure which deviates significantly from the standard, disproportionate build, short and too high in places, and oversized structure as well as hindquarters which are too high.

Great importance is attached to flaws which result from undesirable head traits, such as disproportionately wide or narrow skull and forehead; pointed, hollow or cone-shaped head; hound-head, overly pronounced stop; short, pointed muzzle and ram's head. Major flaws include pendulous lips, loose skin on the head, small, disproportionate, close eyes that are expressionless or have an ill-intentioned expression. Too low or too high-set, narrow, twisted ears.

Teeth which do not lock evenly, undershot bite or an overshot bite over 2 mm, wry mouth and buck-teeth, scale, yellow teeth; pronounced dewlaps on the neck.

The trunk: Slack muscles, loose back and narrow pelvis; short, sway-back or steep hindquarters. Sagging or sunken withers, slack shoulders, chest which is not sufficiently deep or too wide, flat ribs. In the case of bitches sagging belly after whelping.

The limbs: Set of legs deviating from the standard, incorrect angulation. Loose, not closed, long paws.

The tail: Set too high and held considerably higher than the horizontal.

The coat: Thin, silky, extremely short, fine or thin like mouse hair; any deviation from short hair.

The colour: Dark brown, rusty and pale yellow shades are not desirable. A dark stripe on the back (the king stripe), which is often due to nutritional factors, is not considered a major flaw. White spots on the chest or occasionally on the throat and white marks are faulted only if larger than 5 cm in diameter.

Disqualifying flaws: Considerable deviation from the breed characteristics. Deviation from the standard height of over 4 cm, either way. Particolour, spottiness, large white spots on chest, white paws. Pointed foreface, narrow greyhound-like or rough, hound-like skull. Light-coloured or grey eyes and eyes of two different colours. Ectropy, entropy. Strong ram's nose, pink, black and spotted nose, respectively, black pigmented lips or eyelids. Undershot; overshot exceeding 2 mm; wry mouth, pendulous lips, salivation, pronounced dewlaps. Colour lighter than wax-yellow or brown. Shy, weak-nerved albino, cryptorchid or monorchid dogs. Seriously constrained faulty gait. Diagnosed dysplasia of the hip-joint.

The Standard of the Wire-haired Hungarian Vizsla

Name: Wire-haired Hungarian Vizsla, FCI standard No. 239/b, 1982

General Features, Use

Medium-size, strong built, yellow, wire-haired gundog, with bones that are somewhat stronger than those of the short-coated ones. It is somewhat stronger and resistant to cold and water and thus preferred for working in water. In spite of being more robust it resembles the short-coated ones in elegance. It is intelligent, affectionate, well-balanced.

The wire-haired Vizsla was developed in the 1930's, with the German wire-haired pointer figuring importantly in that development. The selective breeding work that went on for decades emphasized form as well as working ability, since the aim was to develop a multi-purpose, hard working Vizsla breed. After this objective had been accomplished, in the breeding process, breed lovers primarily sought to achieve further homogeneity in the texture of the coat and also strove to improve this characteristic in the form. It is closest to the short-coated Hungarian Vizsla in character since it is easy to handle, a quick learner and sensitive to rough treatment. It has good scenting powers, is especially fond of working in water, and retrieves at command. Its style, vigorousness and pointing places this breed on par with continental short-coated pointers.

The head: Well-proportioned, the skull is moderately wide and slightly domed, the foreface is a bit shorter than the skull, the stop is moderate, the arches of the eyes are strong, the characteristic coating makes the head marked, somewhat square. The bridge of the nose is straight to the wide nasal base. The jaw is developed, well-muscled, the teeth are powerful with a scissor-bite. The lips are moderately tight, but not pendulous. The expression is vivid, intelligent, the eyelids are tight, the eyes slightly oval.

The colour of the eyes matches the coat, with a darker colour considered desirable. The ears are set at medium height and are of medium length, covering the ear holes well.

The neck: medium-length, well-muscled, slightly arched, free from disturbing dewlaps.

The trunk: robust and well-proportioned, longer than that of quadratic breeds; the withers pronounced and well-muscled. The back is short and straight, the loin taut; the upper line rounds slightly at the base of the rump. The chest is well-developed, deep and extends at least as far as the elbows. The ribs are moderately arched, the shoulders are well-muscled. The shoulder blades should be suitably slanted and capable of free movement.

The limbs: The forelegs are straight, strong-boned with elbows close to the body. The hindlegs are well-muscled, moderately angled with somewhat low-set

87 Wire-haired Vizsla with an elegant head

88 Wire-haired Vizsla bitch, ideal type and coat
89 Six-week-old wire-haired Vizsla puppies
90 Two-year-old, excellent wire-haired Vizsla stud dog

91 Wire-haired Vizsla dog, excellent type and coat

92 Wire-haired Vizsla bitch
93 Wire-haired Vizsla bitch with a good construction

100 Two-month-old short-haired Vizsla puppies
101 Short-haired Vizsla dog of excellent shape
102 Four-week-old short-haired Vizsla puppy

96 Seven-week-old short-haired Vizsla puppy of the right type
97 Six-week-old short-haired Vizsla puppy
98 Six-month-old short-haired Vizsla puppies
99 Eight-week-old short-haired Vizsla puppy

94 Wire-haired Vizsla bitch retrieving pheasant

95 World champion (beauty) short-haired Vizsla bitch. A really noble, elegant type

103 Four-year-old brood bitch
104 Short-haired Vizsla puppy, "dropping" already perfect

105 Short-haired Vizsla kept as a pet

106 Four-year-old short-haired Vizsla dog pointing game

107 Testing pointing Vizsla puppy with a rabbit

108 Short-haired Vizsla bitch, the ideal type, with a correctly carried pheasant

109 An ambitious Vizsla bringing down a cock pheasant stuck in the branches of a tree

110 When the gun is lifted the dog must drop
111 Getting young Vizslas accustomed to water

112 Even the short-haired Vizsla is willing to work in icy water
113 Well-trained short-haired Vizslas correctly delivering cock pheasant
114 Four-year-old, "laureate" champion short-haired Vizsla bitch, delivering wild duck

115 Some Vizslas can also be used when hunting wild boar

116 Well-trained short-haired Vizsla puppy carrying snipe correctly

117 Vizsla patiently awaiting its master beside the bag
118 Fourteen-year-old, short-haired Vizsla dog, with a stag
119 A good bag

XXI Seven-week-old wire-haired Vizsla puppy

XXII Excellent type three-year-old, short-haired Vizsla
XXIII Short-haired Vizsla family
XXIV Short-haired Vizsla of a world champion family

XXV Short-haired Vizsla with a wild
     duck

XXVI Short-haired Vizsla pointing hare
XXVII Team-work retrieving

XXVIII World champion short-haired Vizsla bitch

XXIX Agár (Hungarian Greyhound) with excellent head

XXX Well-proportioned Agár
XXXI Four-year-old Transylvanian Hound

hocks. The toes are strong, well-arched, close to each other, and the paws are slightly oval. The nails are strong, the pads hard.

The tail: set slightly low, medium thick, tapering towards the end. Docked one-third of its length.

The skin: pigmented, taut, without wrinkles or holds. The nose is flesh-coloured, the lips, edges of the eyelids and nails are brown. The pads are slate-grey.

The hair: short and rough at the foreface with a small bear on the chin. Short and rough on the top of the head. The hair on the ears approximately resembles that of the short-coated Hungarian Vizsla. The hair at the eyebrows is dense and hard. On the neck and the trunk there is a 2–4 cm long, wiry, hard outer coat lying close to the body with an undercoat.

The coat is shorter at the lower end of the limbs and on the lower part of the chest and belly. At the back edges of the limbs longer hair is permissible. The whole make-up of the coat should protect against adverse weather conditions and injuries. On the paws and between the toes the hair is shorter and softer. The tail is covered with a dense, thick coat. The colour of the coat is different shades of sandy yellow. Small white spots on the chest and the end of the feet, as well as white hairs are not faulted.

The gait: vigorous, harmonic, and far-reaching; this breed works and hunts with a balanced, medium-pace canter.

The height: The ideal height (measured with a stick) is

males: 58–62 cm

bitches: 54–58 cm

A deviation of 3 cm either way is permissible, as long as the dog's proportions stay in harmony.

Static and dynamic balance and symmetry are much more important than proportions measured in centimetres.

Type-flaws, defects: Structural flaws or significant defects include anything that adversely affects the harmony of movement and ability to work continuously. Major flaws are an extremely light or rough structure which deviates significantly from the standard; disproportionate build, short and too high in inappropriate places, and oversized structure as well as hindquarters that are too high. Great importance is attached to flaws which result from undesirable head traits such as disproportionately wide or narrow skull and forehead; stop which is too strong; hollow or cone-shaped head; hound-head; overly pronounced stop; short, pointed foreface; and a ram's head.

Major flaws include pendulous lips, loose skin on the head, small, disproportionate eyes which are close and deep-set, an ill-tempered or void expression. Ears set too low or high which are narrow and twisted.

Teeth that do not lock evenly; undershot; overshot exceeding 2 mm and buck tooth; scale, yellow teeth. Dewlap on the neck.

The trunk: Slack muscles; loose back and loin, narrow pelvis, short, sway-back or steep hindquarters, sagging or sunken withers, loose shoulders; chest which is insufficiently deep or two wide, flat ribs. In the case of females, sagging belly after whelping.

The limbs: All fours deviating from the standard with unsuitable angulation. Loose paws which are not close.

The tail: badly docked or curling upwards.

The coat: soft, thin, long, wavy hair. Lack of undercoat. Too short and thin hair on the head, limbs or sides, on the lower part of the belly and chest. Curly or griffon hair, woolly hair on the head are faulted. Major flaw: hair which parts along the backbone.

The colour: dark brown, rusty or pale yellow shades are undesirable. A dark-stripe on the back (the king stripe), which is often due to nutritional factors, is not considered a major flaw. White hairs or white spot on chest or occasionally on the throat are faulted only if larger in diameter than 5 cm.

Disqualifications. Considerable deviation from the breed characteristics. Deviation in height of more than 3 cm in either way from the standard. Parti-colour, spottiness, large white spots, white spots, white paws. A pointed foreface, narrow, greyhound-like or rough, hound-like skull. Very light or grey eyes, eyes of two different colours. Ectropy, entropy. Strong ram's nose, slate-grey, black and spotted nose, respectively and black pigmented lips or eyelids.

Undershot; overshot exceeding 2 mm, wry mouth, pendulous lips, salivation, pronounced dewlap. Colour lighter than wax-yellow or brown colour. Shy, weak-nerved, albino, cryptorchid or monorchid dogs. Seriously constrained, faulty gait. Long, wavy, silky, curling coat. Diagnosed dysplasia of the hips.

The Standard of the Agár, the Hungarian Greyhound (1972)

The Agár is an ancient breed, which probably came with the first Magyar settlers across the Carpathians in the 9th century. Unfortunately, from the 19th century on there has been a lot of interbreeding with imported English Greyhounds, which has tended to mask some of the characteristic features of the original breed.

The Magyar Agár is a tireless, tough hunting dog, a model of speed, power and endurance, which not only catches hares but also attacks bigger game.

It is easy to keep as it is tough, undemanding and bears up well to the extreme temperature variations of its homeland. It is also suited to the racetrack, especially on long distances, being more a coursing dog than a sprinter.

In character it is somewhat reserved but good-natured, intelligent, devoted and even has guarding instincts.

General Features, Use

Frame somewhat oblong. Neither too coarse nor too weedy. Well developed muscles, heavy bone, long sinewy legs.

The head: wedge-shaped from top as well as side aspect. The skull full, the forehead fairly large. Powerful jowls. The muzzle should not be too sniply. Full dentition with strong bite. Lips and nostrils should be dark.

The eyes: of medium size, possibly dark, their expression keen.

The ears: very mobile, of medium size, not so soft as those of the Greyhound. Set fairly high, tilted back in "V" shape or rose-shaped. Permanently pricked up ears are not desirable.

The neck: powerful, of medium length, with an elegant arch and well set to the shoulders.

The body: very muscular hindquarters. Chest deep and capacious, providing ample room for heart and lungs. Flanks slightly tucked up. Back solid but springy, rather straight, only slightly arched at the powerful loins.

The tail: long, not stringy. Carried low, slightly curved.

The forequarters: shoulders oblique, well laid back. Elbows free. Forelegs long and straight. Paws firmly planted on the ground, of moderate length. Strong pads.

The hindquarters: thighs and second thighs wide and muscular, showing great propelling power. Stifles well bent. Hocks powerful, inclining neither outwards nor inwards.

The gait: elegant, springy and dynamic. The Agár is also a good jumper.

The coat: short and close but fairly rough; with some undercoat.

The colour: all colours and colour variations admitted, e.g. plain, spotted, brindle, etc.

The height: males should reach at least 63 cm, bitches 60 cm. No upper limit.

The Standard of the Transylvanian Hound

Name: Transylvanian Hound, FCI Standard No. 241/a, 1963

General Features, Use

A middle-sized, tough hound. Good-natured, courageous, enduring, with an excellent scent. Easy to train.

Form and carriage, proportions, the strong and muscular limbs as well as the set of its tail are characteristic of the Central-European beagle types.

The Transylvanian Hound is bred in two varieties: short-legged and long-legged. The difference between these is in size, colour and hair. The long-legged variety is mostly black, with a coarser and more dense coat; the short-legged one is reddish in colour.

It is an ancient Hungarian beagle-breed, crossed with eastern hounds and also with other Hungarian hunting breeds, however the impact of latter is negligible. The long-legged Transylvanian hound is used to hunt big game (boar, for example).

The short-legged one can be most successfully used for hunting fox and hare. They both have a strong passion for hunting. They are excellent at beating, but also for trailing and retrieving. While driving game the hound gives tongue. It yelps deer to a standstill. Loyal to its master it is ready to protect him.

The head: Rather long beagle head, not tapering. The cranial part is slightly arched. Lips well covering the teeth. Scissors bite. Strong, well-developed teeth.

The eyes: Medium sized, oval in shape, set somewhat obliquely. Dark brown, eyelids closing tight.

The ears: Set middle high. Hanging close to the cheeks without wrinkling. The skin broadens slightly at the middle, then narrows to the rounded ends. When pulled forward the ears just cover the eyes.

The neck: Set medium high, muscular, medium long. On the lower edge, the skin is slightly wrinkled. Slight dewlap not objectionable.

The forelegs: Rather steep, supporting the trunk like columns. Front medium wide. Paws round, compact. Big pads, hard, elastic. Strong nails are black.

The trunk: In the form of a horizontal rectangle. Chest barrel-like and long, not too deep. Well developed withers. The back straight behind the withers. The croup moderately slanting. The belly slightly tucked up.

The stern (tail) is set low, strong at the root, thick and tapering, carried low when in repose, with its end slightly curved upwards. It exceeds the hocks by 1 or 2 cm. While in action, the stern is carried gaily without being curled over the back.

The hindlegs: muscular, the thighs lean. The hocks well set down, the pasterns short. The paws are round, close. Big pads. Strong nails.

The skin and coat: well-pigmented, dark in colour. Nose, lips and eyelids are black. (The nose of the short-legged, red-coated variety may be leather brown).

The coat: short, straight and smooth. The coat of the long-legged variety is somewhat longer, stockier, thicker, it is rough to the touch but shiny. In winter it has some undercoat. The basic colour of the long-legged variety is black. Often there are white spots on the forehead, the breast, the paws and the end of the tail. Tan or rosty markings must be well defined over the eyes, on the side of the jaws, on the upper and perhaps even on the lower part of the limbs. On the parts covered with red hair, black "pencilling" may occur.

The short-legged Transylvanian Hound has a brownish-red basic colour, getting lighter towards the belly and along the limbs. White spots may occur here too on the forehead, the breast, paws, end of tail but these should not be very extended. The muzzle may be "smoky".

The height at withers in the long-legged variety: 55–65 cm.
In the short-legged variety: 45–50 cm.
The weight: 30–35 kg.
The gait: not very fast, but tireless enduring gallop.

About the Work Performed by Hunting Dogs

The breed of hunting dogs to be choosen is always decided by the game to be hunted. From old papers we can read observations that withstood centuries. One of these concerns the question of purity of breed. The following can be read in the already mentioned book written by Diezel-Mika: "Notwithstanding the fact that there still are lots of shooting men who, despising all theories and standing on the ground of practice, are of the opinion that it is not external features that determine the good dog but performance, still, the opinion is slowly gaining ground that a dog of noble origin, besides its pleasing exterior, may be of value in hunting due to its inherited good properties, which not only reduce training work by half but also result in a higher versatility. While out of ten mongrels 2 or 3 will fulfill lesser requirements in hunting work, after arduous training with pure breds the proportion is at least the reverse. There are already quite a number of dogs of pure breed as testified by a pedigree, which gave palpable proof—in different field trials and work competitions—of their suitability both for hunting and breeding."

"Because", continues the book, "a beautiful exterior is not always accompanied by talent in hunting, in the beginning field trials were started to determine the natural inclination of the dogs, their mode of searching, the quality of their nose, their pointing ability and temperament, on which depend to a great measure the success of training. This, in itself, is sufficient for a breeder, but not so for a hunter who wishes to see the work of gun dogs at such a competition and will continue breeding accordingly. For this purpose so-called working dog competitions have been organized where the competing dogs gave proof of their ability to retrieve lost game in difficult circumstances, to track on the leash and without a leash, to bay when finding or lead to a dead game; to show their courage when encountering beasts of prey, how well they can be led on a leash, their quiet behaviour during a break and finally their ability to search in water and in the woods. It was observed during field trials that the best results could be achieved with carefully bred gun dogs. Those who still maintain that also mongrels could be permitted to take part in field trials resemble a blind man speaking about colours."

This opinion of olden times is still a timely question. We can still encounter sportsmen who maintain that mongrels are better gun dogs than any pure bred. Nowadays, when highly specialized and excellent breeds are available for all hunting purposes, it seems unnecessary to produce arguments for the practical use of pure breds, especially Vizslas.

Due to genetical reasons it is of course possible that a mongrel be more intelligent and can be trained more successfully than any of its pure-bred ancestors, from which it originated. However, the good features of the parent-pairs manifest doublefold in the progeny. We may, therefore, say safely that the opinion that a mongrel has a higher hunting value than a pure-bred is just as improbable as a misprint improving the original printed text.

Of gun dogs complete obedience, superb nose, the ability to point and the capability to track are demanded.

Training a hunting dog requires consistence, a great amount of love, patience and steadfastness. A lesson should never last for more than 20 to 25 minutes. An exercise should be repeated several times and it is time to stop when the dog has done it well. The animal should then be praised and given a reward. Never start teaching something new if the former exercise has not been learned to perfection. The presence of onlookers disturbs not only the dog but also its trainer. And remember the basic rule already mentioned: never begin to train your dog under a nervous strain.

Basic Training

The very first thing is to get to know the dog we want to train and to get it to like us. As dogs do not understand the content of words but the intonation only, one ought to try to stick to a timbre when training that permits the dog to draw unmistakeable conclusions. In training, a reward is usually the best method to achieve results. However, disobedience should, if needed, be punished rather severely. In the course of training the objective is that the animal act by itself, hoping for the praise of its master.

Accustoming to walk on a leash is taught with the same methods as already described. Hunting dogs, too, have to walk with their head close to the master's knee. The same rules apply for hunting dogs as for any other breed when teaching them to walk at heel without a leash. Command and praise should alternate.

Teaching to *sit* can be taught either indoors or outdoors. The dog should be called to its master and rewarded with some tit-bit. If the exercise is taught with patience, the young dog will learn it playing, hoping for a praise and a reward.

Down or *drop* can be taught by using a command, a short staccato whistle signal, by lifting our hand, lifting the gun to the shoulder or by the sound of the shot and when a hare jumps up or a pheasant takes wing, respectively. The order of learning is logically the same as that of the above enumeration.

While teaching "down", attention has to be paid that the lying posture be correct. It follows from the command that the dog should not recline on its side or back, it should pull its legs under itself, should not lift its tail. The posture should, therefore, be corrected until the animal achieves regular, quiet "down". The exercise has to be repeated very many times. The dog has to learn to "down" quite unexpectedly, in the most diverse situations. While walking it on a leash, the master should stop all of a sudden and command "down". In the same way, when the dog is not on a leash but at heel, or when at a distance, scenting game, the command "down" should be given. Hunting dogs should also be taught to "down" not only at a spoken command but also when the master gives the signal with his arm or, last but not least, at the sound of an ultra-sound whistle which disturbs game the least.

When a dog has mastered "down" at the sound of a whistle, it should be taught to do the same when at a distance from its master. This needs a leash about 10–15 m long, which, at the beginning, should not be used at full length. Thus, to start with, "down" should be practised with the leash held short and then the master should turn round facing the dog, walking backwards a few steps and lengthen the leash. The leash should not be tight or else the dog may misunderstand us and try to get up. While enlarging the distance, the dog should be kept in sight all the time and the command "down, stay" repeated if it shows signs of getting up. The method aims at teaching the dog to "down" while at heel but also when at a distance and remain in this position until no other command is given. Do not forget to praise and reward your dog each time he succeeds in this exercise.

When "down" on a long leash causes no problem anymore, it is time to start teaching it without a leash. This enables to increase both the time of "down" and the distance between us and the dog. Of course, when the ground is frosty, the dog should not be left lying for a long time, or else it will catch cold.

Accustoming the dog to *the sound of a shot* should not be begun with a live cartridge. Let us start by firing a percussion cap, followed by a blank shell, with a lesser amount of powder. The amount of powder can then be increased up to its full quantity. This method aims at accustoming the dog to the sound of a shot without making him frightened. After a time it will show no sign of nevers and fulfill its task, which is to "down" at the sound of a shot.

Teaching to *come at the sound of a whistle,* there are internationally agreed whistle signals valid for any breed of hunting dog. For "come" it is some short signals followed by one long signal. However, the short ones should not be as short as the ones used for "down" and the long one should not be too lengthy. Calling the dog to come by whistle has the same value, regarding scale of points, as "down" commanded with a whistle.

Commanding "come" by whistle can also be taught later when the dog lies at a certain distance out of sight and then blowing the whistle. If the dog gets up and starts to look for the spot the sound came from and comes to us, he deserves both praise and a reward.

Retrieving and searching for game. Untiring inclination to retrieve is a basic feature of gun dogs. This, of course, makes learning to retrieve much easier. The method is to start by bowling a ball so that the puppy see it rolling along. We will notice that it immediately starts to run after the ball, takes it into its mouth and tries to take it to its bed. If we succeed in making the puppy come close catching it, expressing pleasure and at the same time taking the ball gently from its mouth, taking care that the animal should see the ball in our hand, it will try to get it again. If the ball is bowled another time, the puppy will run after it, and so on. Now the puppy should be made to "down" and permitted only a little later to run after the ball at the same time the command "bring" should be given. If, at the rolling of the ball, the animal tries to jump, "down" is to be repeated and the animal pushed to a lying position. Only when it stayed in this posture for a few moments, should the permit be given to chase after the ball. It is evident that such a permit makes it happy. When the puppy comes to us, it is to be made to sit down. If it does not do so at a command, it should be forced to sit, by pushing down its rear. Only then should the ball be taken from its mouth. This is followed by praise and reward.

Any exercise should only be repeated while the dog is willing. When at the height of success, stop. Time should be given for playing and resting and then, after some hours, the formerly taught exercise can be repeated. Too long "exercise-hours" are tiring and may bore the dog so that it does not respond.

When the dog has mastered an exercise in its home, it is time to take it to an unknown environment, and repeat the exercise there, with a gradually increasing precision. This has a psychological effect as, in an unknown environment, the dog attaches itself even more to its master than at home, out of fear of losing him. Let the animal run around for a while, command "down", throw the ball so that it sees it. Now wait a short time and then give the command "bring" or "fetch". If the dog takes the ball but does not bring it, its master should start walking in the opposite direction and call the dog. If it still does not come, it is best to start running, as, because of the unknown surroundings, the dog will start to run after us. Before accepting the ball, the dog should be made to sit. Now comes praise. However, contrary to other exercises, the rewarding tit-bit should never be given the moment the animal brings the object he was commanded to do so, or else it will be induced to drop it, just to get the reward as soon as possible.

If retrieving a ball causes no difficulties anymore, the ball can be changed for a piece of wood with a hare-skin tied around it. Its strong smell of game is especially liked by Vizslas and retrieved with pleasure. The terrain from where the dumbbell is retrieved should be gradually more difficult. The exercise should

121 Agár bitch with pups
122 Young Agár dog

123 Well-built Agár dog
124 Two-year-old Agár dog
125 Parade before a Greyhound race
126 The Start

127–129 The Race
130 Prize awarding
131 Three-year-old Agár bitch

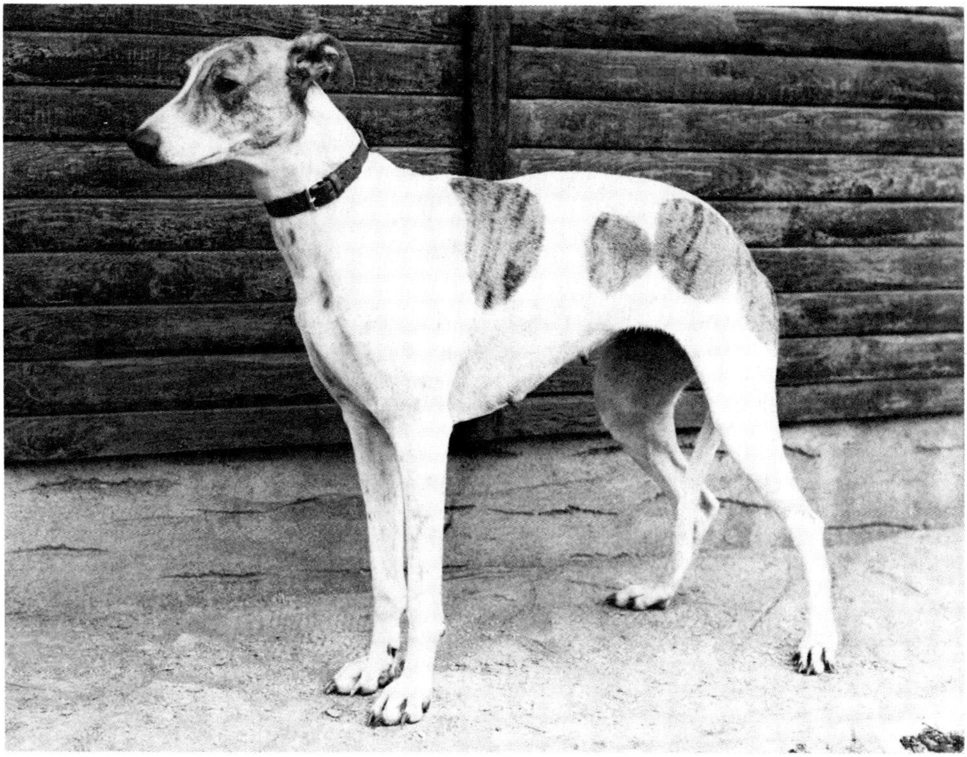

132 Agár bitch with fine bone structure
133 The Agár, the Hungarian Greyhound, is an excellent jumper
134 Transylvanian Hound puppies
135 Transylvanian Hound bitch

13 Transylvanian Hound family

be practised both ways: against wind and with a tail-wind blowing. The distance from where it is to be brought back should be increased gradually.

Searching for game. Dogs working in the field, searching for game, as for instance Vizslas, Pointers, Setters and Spaniels, have the jobs to find game with the least exertion and ensure that no game remain in cover in this terrain. All these dogs find game by its scent. The scent is smelled strongest when it comes in the direction of the wind. Thus the mode of searching is best when the dog proceeds in a zig-zag line, against the wind direction. The intensity of scent greatly depends on the weather and the ground cover. In dry weather the dog will search with less result, while in wet weather the fur or feathers emit a stronger scent, thus results will be better. But of course, searching by scent offers very little opportunity in a tempest or strong rain. Learning the method of searching is part of the basic training of a gun dog. Should the dog not be too interested to search, it is a good method to throw something in the direction we want it to continue the search. When it runs there, another object is thrown in another direction indicating where it ought to continue. Later on nothing is thrown but the movement of throwing is simulated and, commanding "search" we point to the terrain we want to be scoured.

Should game jump up or fly off while practising, this is an excellent occasion to practise "down" with the dog.

Pointing. One of the best features of Vizslas and other gun dogs is that they point the game and thus reveal its presence to the hunter. Pointing usually seems like an unfinished, hesitant step. The moment the game moves, the dog should be commanded to "drop" and be kept in this position for a while. After praising the animal, it ought to be taken on a leash for a time and let free only when quiet. Then it can start searching in another direction. If such exercises are practised with great patience, the Vizsla will get accustomed not only to down at a command, but at any time when it observes game in motion.

Searching and retrieving shot game. The first game to be retrieved should always be a bird. The dog should stay "down" after the shot, then be praised and sent to search. It is best in the beginning to send him after cold game. For a beginner, retrieving a runner means a special difficulty but suitable practise will certainly bring good results.

When the dog, while hunting for big game finds the dead game, it will recoil first. This is the most suitable moment to induce it to "give tongue". This is done by commanding "bark" to indicate that it found the shot game. In case the dog starts to tear at the game, this should be forbidden by repeating "no". After every exercise at least one hour rest should follow.

Working in water is divided into two parts: flushing and retrieving from water. Flushing means that the dog has to go over the reedy, swampy terrain and rouse and put any game. If it points winged game in shallow water it should be encouraged by the command "go off" to put it up. Never permit the dog to bounce after the game.

Dogs, of course, have to get accustomed to working in water. Practising is best begun in shallow water, and the dumbbell wrapped in game skin should be thrown from an increasing distance. If the dog is willing, it will also be ready to swim after game. Vizslas ought to be taught to work in reedy terrain as well this being part of their task.

And what cannot be stressed too often: praise and reward your dog for work done well.

Training the Greyhound for Races

The basis of training Greyhounds is essentially the same as the discipline-training for other breeds. Accustoming our dog to absolute obedience, and keeping it well are requirements necessary even if we do not want to compete with our pet. Any further special training—e.g. the systematic development of the herding ability of shepherd dogs, teaching special tasks to watch dogs—can be based only on discipline. And this, of course, also refers to the special training of racing Greyhounds, which is but the further development of the specific characteristics of the breed, i.e. to make it concentrate on racing.

To keep a Greyhound in training demands lots of time as it is not sufficient to teach the dog how to jump from the box, how to start after the mechanical hare, how to behave on the tracks, etc., as the animal will stay a competitive runner only if kept in constant training. This requires daily exercise. Thus systematic practice just as with sportsmen, is a basic requirement to achieve good results with our Greyhounds.

The selection of a racing Greyhound has to begin at puppy age. A clumsy, shy puppy, with its tail between its legs will never make a good racing dog, or at least very seldom. Brightness, good common sense, quick reflexes, temperament but also a good constitution characterise the puppy that can be trained to become a good runner. Special attention should be paid to correct posture, as any movement of the legs not parallel to the direction of running will slow down the speed. Thus a too narrow posture, a barrel-rear or cow-hockedness, splay toes are all bad faults and if they are inherited features the puppy should never be allowed later for breeding purposes.

Prior to sixth months the puppy should be allowed to play and not be encumbered with serious training. However, it ought to be taught basic discipline, e.g. to stay, to go off, to come to us when called, and of course the dog should be accustomed to its name, to follow on the leash and even without it, and to wear a muzzle.

The dog should be acquainted with the artificial hare even before being introduced to the race track. For this purpose it is best to tie a piece of white fur to a short string, and to draw it slowly in front of it. An indifferent dog will not try to catch the piece of fur while a Greyhound with the makings of a good runner will gaze at it first and then jump. If possible, the dog should never be let to catch the artificial hare. While holding the dog on the leash, the exercise should be repeated in play, encouraging the animal. If we feel sure that its wish to catch the piece of fur is intense, it is time to take off the leash and let the animal jump after the "hare". Later on the fur with the string can be attached to a long stick and turned around in big circles while the puppy runs after it. If the puppy likes this play there is strong hope that it will make a good racing Greyhound. When the puppy is interested and is ready to run after the hare, the moment has arrived to put on a muzzle, since in its excited state, it will not bother about the muzzle but concentrate on the hare.

When the puppy is over 6 months old and its eagerness to catch the hare has been sufficiently awakened while playing, it can be taken to the practising track. In the beginning it will acutely dislike the starting-box, however the following great event will make up for the momentary captivity and later will be impatient to be led to the starting-boxes. However, attention should always be paid never to leave it for too long in the trap. While it has to suffer captivity, it is expedient to encourage it by pulling or moving the "hare" up and down in front of the transparent trapdoors.

The dog should start to run after the hare only after all reflexes are functioning according to our wish. In the beginning the Greyhound should run alone until we are absolutely certain that its only objective is to catch the hare. Later on, while practising, it is best to let it chase the hare in the company of an older, experienced runner, as the presence of the "competitor" will induce it to run even faster.

Racing with Greyhounds has its strict, international rules just as any other sports event.

Coursing with Greyhounds

As already mentioned, the Greyhound never works by scent but by sight. As coursing with Greyhounds is practically extinct on the European continent it is perhaps of interest to tell something about this very interesting and intense mode of hunting.

The training of young Greyhounds was begun at the age of 1 year. The Greyhounds were first accustomed to the leash and then to the saddle, being always on the right hand of the hunter, whether he was on foot or on horseback. During the trainings a brace strung together by twos or a trio (strung together by threes) was always composed in a way that an older more experienced Greyhound was there to teach the new generation. The first practising happened on a flat terrain, covered with grass and poor in game, as far as possible, as game jumping up too frequently might have caused the team to scatter and the greyhounds, coursing on their own, would not have achieved any result.

Thus, the moment a hare jumped up at a suitable distance—about 50 m away —and was sighted by the dogs the hunter or trainer slipping them off the leash made them start after it, commanding "go". The young hounds of course followed the older, more experienced one and the chase started. When the hare felt the leading hound too close it would with a very typical twist change direction and with this the first Greyhound due to his high speed was driven off. Probably the Greyhound which was behind could master the new direction easier. Experienced hounds learned to bracket the hare and force it to turn from one towards the other, thus increasing the opportunity for striking. Once overtaken, a single strike with those superbly strong teeth usually was sufficient to kill the hare. If the terrain was suitable and not too rich in game another coursing could be organised the same day. At the end of the hunt the Greyhounds were taken on the leash and the masters or trainers rode home. The first exercises were practiced, as far as possible, by chasing a young hare and then —as experience grew—with older ones. While training, the experience of success was deemed especially important and thus the terrain was chosen carefully.

When a Greyhound, owing to some special stress, became tired, it "fell behind", returned to its mounted master, and got confined to the saddle. Young Greyhounds were specially protected from over-stressing. "Solo Greyhound" was the name of a dog capable for catching a hare all by itself. A "guarding Greyhound" was the name given to the one that protected the kill from its companions, so they should not tear it apart.

A Greyhound was called well trained if it followed its mounted master quietly on the leash, obeyed his call without hesitation, immediately started after the hare and, when finally it made a kill, awaited the hunter beside it. It was regarded as a major fault if a second hare jumping up during the chase confused the Greyhound.*

Hunting with Hounds

Hunting with hounds was an ancient sport also favoured by the Hungarian nobility. In Hungary hunting with hounds was the fashionable sport up till the middle of the 19th century. A good-looking pack was always kept on country estates. Fashion and the competitive spirit gave rise to the breeding of different kinds of hounds.

According to contemporary documents hunting with a pack was only permitted in the mountains, where game was scarce. Only three were used. The best time for hunting was October in pine forests and in deciduous forests when the trees lost their foliage. A warm, dry weather and dry soil held footmarks and

---

* Kirschler, F.: *Der Jagdhund;* Diezel-Mika: *A vadászebek* (Hunting Dogs), Athenaeum, Budapest, no date of publication.

scent for a shorter time, while humidity and fresh snow eased the work of the pack.

Hunting with hounds is done in groups, on horseback. The guns block the path of the game and the master of the hounds, who has to know the country well, will let slip one or two good hounds first. The moment one of them gives tongue, the others are loosened too. An experienced hunter will know from the sound of baying whether the hounds follow a cold or still warm scent, whether they are near to the game, whether they chase by sight, and whether they have caught or stopped the game. The first "music" can usually be heard at certain distances except when the game jumped up directly before the dogs. The baying of a pack of beagles is regarded as the loveliest music by those riding to hounds. In this context an anecdote deserves to be told about a gentleman, who was not a hunter accompanying a friend of his on a hunt with beagles.* "Some moments after arriving at our place" writes the hunter, "I already heard the sound of my three beagles and the nearer they came, the forest echoed with their baying. Do you hear that heavenly music? I whispered to my friend. But there he stood, both hands on his ears answering dejectedly: Where? I cannot hear anything, these hounds make a such awful noise!"

* Diezel-Mika; Op. cit.

BIBLIOGRAPHY

Dr. Lajos Abonyi: *A kutyák ápolásáról* (The Routine Care of Dogs). Budapest, Springer, 1935

Abonyi—Anghi—Kukuljevics—Vajda: *Amit a kutyáról mindenkinek tudnia kell* (What Everybody Should Know about Dogs). Országos Egészségügyi Egyesület, Budapest, 1958

A Magyar Puli küllemi bírálata (The Show Judging of Hungarian Pulis). Hungarian Standard 6811 — T. Budapest, 1966

Dr. Csaba Anghi: *A magyar pásztorkutyák terminológiája, jellegleírása és standardja* (The Terminology, Description and Standard of Hungarian Sheep Dogs). *Debreceni Szemle,* Debrecen, 1935. IV. No. 4

Dr. Csaba Anghi: *A magyar pásztorkutyák* (Hungarian Sheep Dogs). *Természettudományi Közlöny,* 1935. No. 67

Dr. Csaba Anghi: *Die ungarischen Hirtenhunde.* Paul Schöps, Leipzig, 1938

Dr. Csaba Anghi: *Pásztorkutyáink* (Our Sheep Dogs). *Búvár,* 1936. No. XII

Dr. Csaba Anghi: *A nagy pásztorkutyák és a külföldi rokonfajták* (Hungarian Sheep Dogs and Related Foreign Dogs). Budapest, Springer, 1936

Állattenyésztési enciklopédia (Encyclopedia of Animal Husbandry). Vols. I–III. Budapest, Mezőgazdasági Kiadó, 1959

Gyula Balázs: *A kutya fogainak rendellenességei, betegségei és életkorának meghatározása* (Anomalies in the Teeth of Dogs, Diseases and Determination of Age). Hornyánszky Viktor RT. Budapest, 1935

Bertus, F. J.: *Novus Orbis Pictus* (Természethistoriai Képeskönyv). Wien, 1805. Published by Antal Pichler.

Andor Biró—János Győri: *Kutyakiképzési Kézikönyv* (Handbook of Dog Training). Budapest, Mezőgazdasági Kiadó, 1971

Alfred Brehm: *Az állatok világa* (The World of Animals). (Hungarian Translation) 1907, Budapest, Légrády printing shop.

Alfred Brehm: *Az állatok világa* (The World of Animals). Vols. I–V. (Hungarian translation) Budapest, Guttenberg, 1923

Géza Buzzi: *A magyar juhász- vagy pásztorebek* (Hungarian Sheep or Herding Dogs). *A természet.* Budapest, 1915. No. 5

Géza Buzzi: *Végakkordok a juhászebek elnevezése körül* (The End of the Dispute Regarding the Name of Sheep Dogs). *Állattenyésztési és Tejgazdasági Lapok.* Budapest, 1909, No. 5

Géza Buzzi: *A hazai pásztorebek regenerációja* (Regeneration of the Hungarian Sheep Dogs). *Állattenyésztési és Tejgazdasági Lapok.* Budapest, 1907. No. 7.

Amos Comenius: *Janua linguae Latinae reserata aurea,* in hung. linguam translata per Stephanum Beniamin Szilágyi. Kolozsvár 1673

Diezel—Mika: *A vadászebek* (Hunting Dogs). Athenaeum, Budapest. No date of publication

Dorn, F. K. dr.: *Hund und Umwelt.* Deutscher Bauernverlag. Berlin, 1957

Henrik Dorning: *Régi irodalmi adatok a komondorról* (Ancient Literary Data on the Komondor). *Pótfüzetek a Ter-*

mészettudományi Közlönyhöz. Királyi Magyar Természettudományi Társulat. Budapest, 1915. No, 89

Gyula Éhik: *Új magyar Brehm* (New Hungarian Brehm). Budapest, Gutenberg, 1927

Dr. Lajos Fekete: *A pumiról* (The Pumi). *Kisállattenyésztés* 1961. No. 2

Fitzinger: *Sitzungsberichte* (Report). *Akademie*. Wien LVI. October, 1867

József Fónagy: *A vizsla idomítása* (Training the Vizsla). Budapest, Athenaeum 1905

Göckel, H.: *Hundezucht in Wort und Bild*. Verlag Sport und Technik, Berlin, 1956

Dr. József Hajas—dr. Pál Sárkány: *Bobbyhobby. Bánásmód kutyákkal képekben* (Bobby-Hobby. Life with Dogs in Pictures). *Natura,* Budapest, 1970

Dr. József Hajas—dr. Pál Sárkány: The New Owner's Handbook. Howell Book House Inc. New York, 1972

János Hanák: *Természetrajz* (Natural History). Pesth, 1848. Vol. 1

Ottó Herman: *Az ősfoglalkozások köréből* (Ancient Crafts). *Természettudományi Közlöny,* Budapest, 1899.

Ottó Herman: *A pásztorok nyelvkincse* (The Language of Shepherds). Természettudományi Társulat, Budapest, 1914

Ottó Herman: *A magyarok nagy ősfoglalkozása* (The Main Primeval Occupation of the Hungarians). Természettudományi Társulat, Budapest, 1909

Dr. Artur Horn: *Általános Állattenyésztés* (General Animal Husbandry). Mezőgazdasági Kiadó, Budapest, 1955

Lajos Ilosvay—Hollósy: *A kutya* (The Dog). Budapest, Athenaeum, 1921

Lajos Ilosvay—Hollósy: *A magyar nemzeti kutyafajták fajtajellegének leírása* (Description of Type of Hungarian Breeds). Magyar Ebtenyésztők Országos Egyesülete, Budapest, 1936

Zoltán Kenéz: *A komondor meghatározása és a pásztoreb leírása* (Standard of the Komondor and Description of Sheep Dogs). Edition Daróczy, Túrkeve, 1922

Dr. Ernő Kubinszky—György Szél: *A kutya* (The Dog). Mezőgazdasági Kiadó Budapest, 1956

Konrad Lorenz: *So kam der Mensch auf den Hund*. Hungarian translation: Gondolat, Budapest, 1973

Konrad Lorenz: *Der Ring des Solomon*. Hungarian translation: Gondolat, Budapest, 1973

Sándor Lovassy: *A magyar pásztorkutyák* (Hungarian Sheep Dogs). *Természettudományi Közlöny,* Budapest, No. 26. 1919

Dr. Erna Mohr: *Ungarische Hirtenhunde*. Ziemsen Verlag. Wittemberg, Lutherstadt, 1956

Károly Monostori: *Ebtenyésztés* (Dog Breeding). Franklin Társulat, Budapest, 1909

A kutya tenyésztése, tartása és kiképzése (Breeding, Keeping and Training of Dogs). Ed. Dr. Pál Sárkány. Mezőgazdasági Kiadó, Budapest, 1972

Dr. Imre Ócsag: *Magyar őrző és terelő kutyák* (Hungarian Guarding and Herding Dogs). Debrecen, 1985

Dr. Imre Ócsag: *A puli* (The Puli). Mezőgazdasági Könyvkiadó, Budapest, 1962

Dr. Imre Ócsag: *Puli vagy Pumi* (Puli or Pumi). *Kisállattenyésztés,* 1961, No. 3

Dr. Imre Ócsag: *Puli tenyész-szemle Debrecenben* (Puli Show in Debrecen). *Kisállattenyésztés,* Budapest, 1961. No. 1

Dr. Imre Ócsag: *Mely elvek alapján végezzük a kutyák kiválasztását* (Principles of Selecting Dogs.) *Élővilág*. 1964. 9. No. 1

Dr. Imre Ócsag: *Milyen színű legyen a puli* (What Colour Should a Puli Be). *Élővilág,* 1964. 9. No. 6

F. Páriz Pápai: *Dictionarium Latino-Hungaricum*. Tyrnaviae, 1762

Ferenc Pethe: *Természethistória és mesterségtudomány* (Natural History and Professional Sciences). Nemzeti Gazda Hivatal, Vienna, 1815

Gábor Prónay: *Vázlatok Magyar Hon népéletéből* (Sketches from the Life of Hungary). Pesth, 1855

Emil Raitsits: *A magyar eb* (The Hungarian Dog). *A természet,* Budapest, 1916

Emil Raitsits: *A magyar kutyák* (Hungarian Breeds). Centrum, Budapest, 1924

Emil Raitsits: *A magyar juhászkutyák bírálata* (Judging Hungarian Sheep Dogs). *A természet,* Budapest, 1920. Nos. 15–16

Emil Raitsits: *A komondor, kuvasz, puli* (The Komondor, the Kuvasz, the Puli). Pátria, Budapest, 1917

Emil Raitsits: *A magyar juhászkutyafajták leírása. Standard.* (Description of Hungarian Sheep Dogs). *A természet,* Budapest, 1921, Nos. 5–6

Emil Raitsits: *Pumitenyésztésünk* (Breeding of Pumis). *A természet,* Budapest, 1928

Dr. Pál Sárkány: *Einheitliche Richteransicht und das FCI Standardenbuch* (Lecture held in German. World Cynology Congress. Dortmund, 1973)

Miksa Scholtz: *Kanászó ebeink minősége* (Our Boar Hounds). *Vadászlap,* 1884, p. 117

Dr. János Szigeti: *A háziállatok korszerű szelekciója* (Modern Selection of Domestic Animals). Mezőgazdasági Kiadó, Budapest, 1959

Antal Szirmay: *Hungaria in Parabolis.* Pesth, 1807

János Szunyoghy: *A puli tudománya* (About the Puli). *Természettudományi Közlöny,* 1940, vol. 72. No. 1109

Friederick Treitschke: *Naturhistorischer Bildersaal des Thierreiches.* Pesth und Leipzig, Verlag von C. A. Hartleben, 1840

Dr. Ágoston Zimmermann: *Háziállatok anatómiája* (Anatomy of Domestic Animals). Esztergom, Gusztáv Buzárovics, 1923